THE BLENDER 3D COOKBOOK, V

By Ira Krakow

Introduction

The Blender 3D Cookbook consists of the scripts to my Blender 3D tutorials, at http://www.youtube.com/irakrakow. Each script has a link to the Youtube video. Many of you have requested such a book. I called the book a "cookbook" because you can think of the scripts as "recipes" for producing a desired effect in Blender.

I don't assume any particular level of Blender expertise. My videos cover a wide variety of topics, from beginner to advanced. Like a cookbook, you can pick and choose those recipes you are interested in and skip the ones that you either know about or that you're not interested in. I tried to include something for everyone, including topics such as the Blender Game Engine and Python scripting that have only been lightly covered in other tutorials. If you have suggestions for future tutorials, please email me at ira.krakow@gmail.com. The tutorials have been updated for Blender 2.62, the most current release version of Blender as of February, 2012.

These tutorials are not intended to cover every conceivable Blender feature. That would, in my opinion, be too thick a volume. Note that I suffixed the title to this cookbook "Volume 1". Blender is too complex and rich a program, undergoing constant upgrading and changing, for that. Hopefully, there will be many more volumes of the Blender 3D Cookbook, in the future, that will explore other amazing and unique Blender features.

User Interface

Default Scene

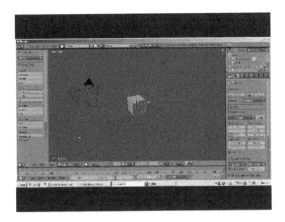

Watch the video at: http://www.youtube.com/watch?v=7cHzsOga-DY

When you first open Blender a number of default windows, panels, and controls, are displayed. At first you might be intimidated by it, but as you become more familiar with the Blender interface, you'll find that the layout is very well organized and provides an efficient interface for modeling and animation. The default layout contains are 5 Blender windows, called editors. Each of these editors contains a header and a menu line. Sometimes the header is at the top, other times at the bottom. Even though you might think of a header at the bottom as a footer, Blender calls it a header.

The first default editor window is called the Information Editor, located at the very top of the display. This window contains just a header line with frequently used commands in menu form. There is information about the scene, object or subobject elements, memory, and selection.

The second editor window is the Outliner Editor, with a small header window, and a small window at the right, as a hierarchical display.

The third editor window is called the Properties Editor. It's a cluster of context buttons, panels, and controls, which control texturing, rendering, lighting and scene objects. I will move the cursor until I see a double arrow. Left click and drag the window to the left to get a better look at it. All Blender windows can be extended this way either horizontally or vertically. The Properties Editor consists of context buttons, similar to tabs, that change

panels and controls below depending on the context. Below the
context buttons are panels that open and close when you click on the
open/close arrows. Inside the panels are controls, which manipulate
the scene based on context, These controls are typically either a
function, option, or value. I'll resize this window based on the
original size.

The fourth editor window is the Timeline editor, at the bottom of the
display, which has a header window that contains animation or
playback controls, and a running timeline that displays the position
of the playback head, with keyframes that you have added to your
animation.

The fifth editor window, which comprises most of the default display,
is the 3D Viewport editor window. This is where you'll concentrate
much of your modeling attention. It consists of a header menu,
located at the bottom of the window, that contains viewing and
selecting controls. On the far left of the 3D editor window are a
number of tool panels for button controls for manipulating selected
objects and adding keyframes. On the right is a large viewing space
for viewing, selecting, and transforming your 3D objects. This 3D
viewing space, which constitutes the visible Blender scene, contains
the default cube object, a lamp object, and a camera object. When I
select any of the objects by right clicking on them, the various
editor windows panels automatically change based on the object being
selected.

It's possible to change the type of the editor window. Click on the
Editor Type button located on the left end of every editor header
menu. For instance, here I will change the 3D editor window the the
File Browser editor window.

Now I will change it to the User Preferences editor window.

Now I will change it back to the 3D Viewport.

The default Blender window can be changed. I suggest you make only
minor changes until you become more familiar with the location of the
editor panels, context buttons, and controls available in Blender.

Splitting And Joining Windows (2.49)

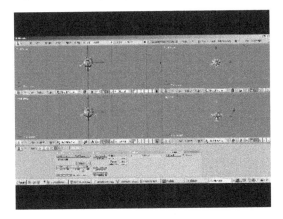

Watch the Video at: http://www.youtube.com/watch?v=uYb1j8X-ulc

Blender's default scene has the following three windows:

- The Preferences Window (at the top)
- The 3D Viewport Window (in the middle)
- The Buttons Window (at the bottom)

It is possible to split and join windows, and to turn the window into a different type, so that you get a different view in that window.

To set up the initial scene, Start up Blender. Then, delete the default cube (right click on the cube to select, then press either the DEL key or X, then Enter).

Finally, add Suzanne, Blender's monkey mascot (SPACE - Add - Mesh - Monkey).

Now we're going to split the 3D Viewport window into 4 windows, to show the top, right side, front, and camera views, at the same time. First, we split the window horizontally, as follows:

Drag the cursor to the extreme left edge of the 3D viewport. The cursor changes to a double sided arrow. When you right click, you get a menu with a choice of No Header or Split Area. Click on Split area.

You will see a horizontal line. The line shows where the 3D window will be split if you left click. You can move the line to control exactly where you want the split to occur. When you are satisfied with the split, left click and the window will split horizontally into 2 windows.

We need 4 windows. We will split each window vertically start with the top 3D window, and drag the cursor to the window's bottom edge. The cursor will change to a double sided arrow, this time pointing vertically. When it does, right click, choose Split Area, and you will see a vertical line showing where the window will be split. The line will be in the window that will be split. When you are at the place where you want the window to split, left click to split the window.

Do the same procedure with the bottom window, until you get 4 windows.

Each window can be switched to a different type. Blender has many types of windows. If you click on the 3D icon, at the lower left side of the window, you can see all the types. Let's switch to the outline window, which shows all the objects in our scene in a table. As you get more comfortable with Blender, you will switch windows often. The outliner is a handy way to switch between different objects in the scene without having to navigate. It helps when the scene becomes complicated. Our scene has, in addition to Suzanne, a camera and a lamp. Click on the outliner icon and change our view back to 3D.

Right now, each window has the same view of Suzanne, the top view, looking at her from the top down. I just happen to know that. Blender can tell us what view we're in, and it's a good idea that you know as well. To display the view orientation, open up the User Preferences window (it has an I, for Information, label, in the upper left corner. Drag on the bottom of the window until you see a double arrow. Left click and drag down until the window opens up. Press the View Names button, on the left row. The button darkens, which is Blender's way of telling you that the feature is active. Then close the window by clicking on the lower left corner and dragging up.

Note that on each window, on the upper left corner, is the phrase "Top Ortho". This means that the window is in Top View, in what's called Orthographic mode. Orthographic mode means that distance is not taken into account and that the size of the object is not distorted by distance. Most of the time you will model in orthographic mode. We'll discover another mode soon.

Using the View Menu of the 3d window, you can change each view to a different perspective. By using the menu, change the first window to Top, the second window to Front, the third window to Right (the default side), and the fourth window to Camera. Now move the monkey, by right clicking on Suzanne to select it (a pink highlight displays), and then pressing the G key and then dragging the mouse. You can see the effect of moving the monkey in each window.

Look at the window that's in camera view. Note that the indicator in the top right corner of the window is "Camera Persp". Persp stands for Perspective view, which means that distance is taken into account. It's like a highway, where parallel lines meet at a long distance. In orthographic mode, the parallel lines will not meet.

There are shortcuts on the numeric keypad for switching to each view. They are:

Top View: NUM7

Front View: NUM1

Side (Right) View: NUM3

Camera View: NUM0

Also, by holding the CTRL key at the same time as pressing the numeric keypad, you get the opposite view. Thus:

Bottom View: CTRL+NUM7

Back View: CTRL+NUM1

Side (Left) View: CTRL+NUM3

CTRL+NUM0 gives you a message "Object as Camera". This lets you view the scene from the perspective of the object, say from Suzanne, the Blender monkey's view.

NUM5 toggles between orthographic and perspective, for any view.

To join windows, drag the cursor to the border of the windows to join. When the cursor changes to a double arrow, Right Click and select Join Areas. You'll see a huge arrow, which tells you in what direction the joining will take place. Press Enter to join the windows. You can join either horizontally or vertically.

One last point. If the view is not one of the standard views, say, you rotate your view using the middle mouse button, or ALT+Left mouse button if you have turned on 3D button emulation in your preferences window, Blender calls that view "User", which means you chose your own special, tilted view.

Splitting and Joining Windows (2.5)

Watch the Video at: http://www.youtube.com/watch?v=AMBi1R7KB48

A big thank you to Neal Hirsig (nhirsig@tufts.edu) of Tufts University. His video, at http://www.gryllus.net, was the source of my video. It is possible to expand an editor window by moving the cursor to the edge of the window until you see a double arrow. Left click and drag the window open. This can be done horizontally or vertically.

You also can split an editor editor into multiple editor windows. To split, place the cursor in the upper right hand corner of the editor window. There's a splitter widget that looks like a ridged thumb grip. When the cursor turns into a cross, left click and drag the cursor horizontally to create a vertical split. You can also create a horizontal split by placing the cursor in the splitter widget until a cross appears, and left clicking and dragging the cursor vertically to create a horizontal split. Each window has its own header window and an associated tool panel.

You can click on the Type button at the far left of the window header menu line. Can change this window to a text editor editor.

You can join two vertical windows with the same width, or any two horizontal windows that have the same height. To join, you can move the cursor on one of the splitter widgets, from one window to the other and make it a joined window. Large grey arrow shows the direction of the change. With the left mouse button pressed, you can drag into either of the windows to join to control the direction of the split. Here I will join two vertical windows into one 3D window.

Notice that each panel inside the editor window also contains a thumb grip splitter widget. So you can join and split the windows you just created. In the case of a panel, you can arrange the placement of the panel within the editor window. Place the cursor on the splitter widget in Layers panel and drag to above the Render Panel. Panels cannot be moved from one editor window to another editor window.

You can also make any blender window full screen. To do that, click in the window to give the cursor focus. Then press CTRL+Down Arrow. That makes it full screen. To make it regular screen press CTRL+Down Arrow again. CTRL+Up works as well. It's a toggle. We'll make the 3D Viewport full screen, and then make it regular screen. We'll make the Outliner window full screen and then revert back to regular size. Switching between full screen and regular size windows will make your modeling much more efficient.

The new 2.5 user interface makes it easy for you to control the size and placement of your windows.

Orientations (2.5)

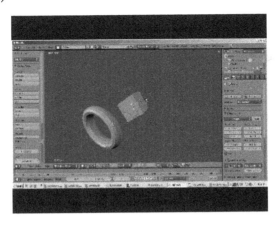

Watch the Video at: http://www.youtube.com/watch?v=eP7G2dC6b4o

The name of this tutorial is Blender 2.5 Global and Local Orientation. Thank you to Near Hirsig (nhirsig@tufts.edu). The tutorial on which is this based is at http://www.gryllus.net. Blender uses 3 dimensions, X in red, Y in green, and Z in blue. The default orientation is global. The orientation remains constant, regardless of which object is selected or which view is active.

Blender allows you to change the X, Y, and Z axis from global to local orientation.

Start with the default Blender scene. Add a torus (SHIFT+A Mesh Torus). In global orientation, the Z axis runs up and down. The Y axis, in green, runs towards and away from the front. The X axis, in red, always runs horizontal to the front.

Switch to Front view (NUM1). Press R key and rotate the torus Y 45 degrees (R Y 45). You can rotate the torus along the global X or Z axis as well.

You can change the axis orientation from global to local by clicking on the Orientation dropdown box. Change the orientation from global to local. The orientation is based on the object's axis. Can rotate the torus along its X, Y, or Z axis, instead of the global X, Y, or Z axis.

Select the cube. We're still in local orientation. However, since the cube was never rotated, the global and local orientations are the

same. Rotate the cube 45 degrees on Y axis (R - Y - 45 - ENTER).
The Translate manipulator widget reflects the object's axes.

Select the torus. Switch from Translate manipulator widget to the
Scale manipulator widget. Scale the torus along local Z axis, or its
local X axis.

Switch to the Rotate manipulator widget. You can also rotate the
torus along local Z axis and local X axis. Since the rotation is
initially around the Z axis and then the X axis, in Front view, we
can see all 3 axes, local blue Z axis, local green Y axis, and the
local red X axis.

Switch to Translate manipulator widget. Rotate the view to a
dimensional user view. With the cube object selected and with the
orientation as local, it makes it easier to manipulate objects along
its axes. Press SHIFT+D to create a duplicate cube. The duplicate
cube moves along the same local axis.

Blender also supports the View orientation, in which the orientation
is the same as the view you are in, either Front, Side, Top, or User.
A new orientation for 2.5 is the Gimbal orientation which is specific
to gyroscopic type objects like a top or a gyroscope.

World Colors (2.49)

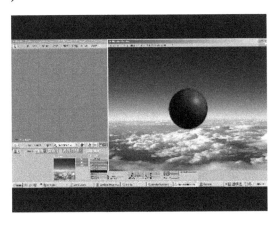

Watch the Video at: http://www.youtube.com/watch?v=zJ1IPr6Y-qk

Blender provides a number of useful settings to set up a background color, image, and texture, as well as the special effects of mist and stars. These settings are important because they interact with many other parts of your scene, such as lamps, materials, and textures on your objects. You need to be aware of how the world settings work even if you don't change them often. The purpose of this tutorial is to explore the one setting you can't miss - the world colors.

First, let's set the scene. Delete the default cube (Right click, press the DEL key, and press Enter to confirm). Add a UV Sphere (Space - Add - Mesh - UV Sphere), accepting the default of 32 segments and 32 rings. Press the Set Smooth button in the Edit panel to smooth out the UV Sphere. Add a subsurf modifier by pressing the Modifiers button and selecting Subsurf. Set the levels to 2. Switch to Front view (NUM1). You know you're in Front view if the blue Z arrow points upward. Make the UV Sphere red by pressing the shading buttons (F5), pressing Add New, and setting R=1, G=0, and B=0.

Press the Home key to see the lamp, the sphere, and the camera. Move the lamp near the camera. Select the lamp first, then the camera, then CTRL+P to make the camera the parent of the lamp. We want to be able to position the camera so that it can track the UV Sphere and we can see the horizon. Go to the Object buttons (F7), then go to the Constraints button, at the far right. Select the Track To constraint. Enter the word Sphere in the Ob: area. Click the -Z button, the last - sign in the To: area, and the Y button in the Up: area. No matter where the camera is positioned, its focus is on the sphere.

Press F12 to render. Note that the sphere is red and the background color is blue. The background color comes from the World color settings, which you get to by pressing F5 (Shading), and then pressing the World icon in the Subcontext area. The preview square shows the default background color, which is derived from the Horizon color - Red=.05, Green=.22, and Blue=.4. Move the camera closer to the ground (the horizontal red line across the window) and press F12 to render. The background color is blue no matter where you position the camera.

There are many ways to change the background color. The first is just to change the horizon color directly. Make the background magenta by setting R=1, G=0, and B=1 for the horizon colors.

That's simple enough. You can also make the background a gradient of two colors, from the top to the bottom. Let's make the background color a gradient, from blue at the top to orange at the bottom. To do that, set the Zenith color to blue (ZeR=0, ZeG=0, and ZeB=1) and the Horizon color to orange (HoR=1, HoG=.5, and HoB=0). Click the Blend button to activate color blending. Press F12 to render. Move the camera around the cube and render. No matter where the camera is positioned, the background is the same blue to orange blend.

Click the Real button. Now there are two gradients. The first, from the zenith (the top) to the horizon, goes from blue to orange. The second goes from the horizon to the nadir (the bottom), from orange to blue. If the camera has the horizon line (the red line in the 3D view) in range, it's rendered as an orange line, as a real horizon. However, if the camera is directly overhead or beneath the horizon, the orange horizon line is not rendered.

Click the Paper button. With all three buttons active, the zenith to horizon to nadir gradient is always rendered, no matter where the camera is positioned.

Of course, if you have a real sky image, you can use it instead of the colors. To do that, you add an image texture. Go to the Texture and Input panel and select the first texture rectangle. Name the texture Sky. Then press F6 to go to the Texture panel. Click the Load Image button. Select the Sky image. Then go back to the World buttons, select the Map To panel, and click on Hori, for Horizon. Press F12 to render. If you click the ZeUp and ZeDown buttons as well, the Sky image is rendered no matter where the camera is positioned.

That's it. I hope this gives you a good grasp of how to use world color settings.

World Background Image (2.49)

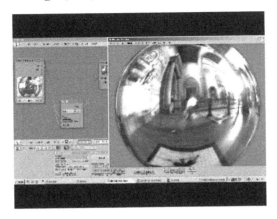

Watch the Video at: http://www.youtube.com/watch?v=vyColc4Uo28

In my tutorial on world background colors, we saw how to change the background color, produce a gradient from one color to another as a background to the scene, and how to map the colors to the world horizon and zenith. Blender also lets you use an entire image, such as a sky image, as a background. In addition, if you turn on Ray Mirror reflection, which I discussed in my Ray Mirror tutorial, you can make objects in your scene reflect the background image so that it appears to exist inside the image generated world. What's interesting is that no lamps are required for this effect. All the light comes from the image itself. This general class of techniques is called Global Illumination, or GI. You can see the dramatic effects of GI in movies such as Avatar, where an entire world is created as the characters fly around inside it. Even though we'll do this on a smaller scale, the principle is the same.

Here are the steps:

1) We'll prepare our fake world first. Start with the default scene. Delete the default cube (Right click, press the DEL key, press Enter to confirm). Select the lamp and delete it the same way. We're going to create a UV Sphere and have it reflect the background. Add a UV Sphere (Space - Add - Mesh - UVSphere). Scale it up 2 times (S - 2 - Enter).

We're also going to add a Track To constraint on the camera. Press the Home key to include all the objects in the scene. Select the camera. Press the Object buttons (F7), then the Constraints button. Select the Track To constraint and make the object the Sphere. Set

Fw to -Z and Up to Y. Our scene is very simple: the UVSphere and the camera.

2) Now let's place an image in the background. Actually, any image will do. As we will see, the higher the image resolution, the more realistic the effect. We'll start with a JPEG of the sky. I downloaded an evening sky jpeg from www.1000skies.com, a good place if you're looking for sky images. You can google Free Sky Images for more.

To make the image the scene background, select F5 for the shading buttons. Click the globe icon for the World buttons. Press the texture button (F6). Make sure that the World texture is selected. Select the top texture channel, click Add New, and from the Texture Type dropdown, select Image. Click Load Image, and load your chosen JPEG. Go back to the World Buttons. In the Preview panel, press Real. In the Texture and Input panel, change the setting to AngMap (Angular Map) to make map to the entire background. In the Map To panel, change the setting to Hori (for Horizon) from the default of Blend. Press F12 to render. The sky renders in the background.

3) This is a start, but we can do better. You can control the size of the background image. From the Texture and Input buttons, increase SizeX and SizeY to 3 to zoom in on the image. Press F12 to render. We get some of the ground as well, if we move the camera so that it can see the ground. One problem is that this JPEG isn't set up to show the entire 360 degree world. The best way is to use an image, called an HDR Image, for High Definition Range, which has a high enough resolution to show the entire 360 degrees of the world we want to simulate. Sometimes they're called Light Probes. If you do a Google Search on Free HDR images, you'll find many HDR images that you can use, not only of the sky, but of buildings, landscapes, mountains, canyons, and so on. I'm using an HDR image of Galileo's tomb in Florence, Italy, from the Light Probe Image Gallery. Google Light Probe Image Gallery to download this and many others. Look for files with the HDR extension. To use this image, go to the World buttons, and then the Texture button. Delete the first image by pressing the X key. Then I click the Load Image button and load the HDR image. In the Texture and Input buttons, set SizeX and SizeY back to 1. Press F12 to render. The new HDR image renders in the background.

4) A really interesting effect can be produced by having our UV Sphere reflect the image, like a crystal ball. To enable this effect, select the Sphere, go to the Shading Buttons (F5),and choose the default material (Material). Go to the Mirror Trans tab. Turn on the Ray Mirror button and set Ray Mirror to 1, which is 100% Ray Mirror. Check out my Ray Mirror tutorial for other effects. For this demo, the ball is getting all of its image information from the

HDR image. Press F12 to render. If we reposition the camera somewhere else, we see a different part of the image, just as if the ball was inside the image.

5) Let's get a panoramic view of our world by animating the camera around the sphere. Clear rotation (ALT+R) and location (ALT+G) on the camera. Press SHIFT+C. Add Bezier circle. Scale it 4 times. Go to Edit Buttons. Press CurvePath to make the Bezier circle a path. Then select the Camera. Delete the track To constraint. Add the Follow Path constraint, making the object CurveCircle, the default name for the Bezier circle. Set Fw to -Z and Up to Y. Add the Track To constraint back. Set the Object to Sphere and Fw to -Z and Up to Y. Press SHIFT+ALT+A to animate. The camera follows the sphere along the circular path. To animate this, go to the Scene buttons (F10), set the end frame to, say, 100, change the output directory to where you want the video file to end up, set the video type (I like AVI compressed, but MOV for quicktime works as well). I'll pause the video while the animation renders. Here's the result: a camera flyaround inside the image.

6) Suppose you want to eliminate the background and just have the sphere reflect the world. Here's how to do it. Go to the World buttons by pressing F5 (Shading), then the World button. Change the window to the Node Editor. Click on the Face Icon (for Composite Nodes), then press Use Nodes. You get the RenderLayer input (our scene), as well as a Composite Node output node (the composite result). Add a Mix Node (Space - Add - Color - Mix). Connect the Image socket of the RenderLayer node to the input Image socket of the Mix node. Connect the Alpha socket of the RenderLayer node to the Fac socket of the Mix Node. Connect the output Image Socket of the Mix node to the Image socket of the Composite node. The background has disappeared, replaced by the color of the first Image socket of the Mix node. You can change the color to anything you want. Make it red, for example. To render the effect, go to the Scene buttons (F10), press the Do Composite button, and press F12 to render. You can redo the animation without the background if you like.

As you can see, you can create your own little Avatar like world in Blender. I hope this gives you some ideas for your own creativity. Be sure to press the Subscribe button in YouTube so you won't miss any of my other tutorials. Happy Blendering!

Append and Link (2.49)

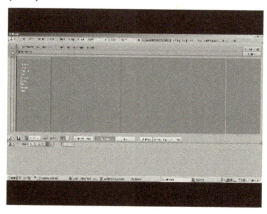

Watch the Video at: http://www.youtube.com/watch?v=69ZBlDrOlIY

Suppose you have created a complicated scene, complete with a neat texture, materials, animations, and whatever else. You might want to reuse the scene, or objects in it, in another blend file. Or, you may be collaborating with others. One person does the textures and materials, another does the animation, a third is setting up the camera, and so on. How can everyone work on his or her own piece of the project and have it all come together in one final blend file? Fortunately, Blender comes to the rescue. Blender has powerful features - called Append and Link - which lets you import all sorts of things from other .blend files into your .blend file. The goal of this tutorial is to show you how you won't have to reinvent the wheel. Instead, you just use Append and Link to reuse what already has been created.

We are first going to create a blend file with some objects, materials, and scenes that you might want to share with others.

1) Select the default cube. The cube has a default material. Go to the F5 (Shading buttons). Click the Generate An Automatic Name button to make the material something descriptive. Blender makes an attempt at creating a realistic name for the material. It's name is now Grey.

2) Add green monkey (Space - Add - Mesh - Monkey). Move the monkey 2 Blender units to the right to separate it from the cube. Press F5 (Shading) and click Add New. Make material green (R=0, G=1, B=0). Name the material something descriptive, using the Automatic Name button. The material is now named LightGreen.

3) Create a new, empty scene by going to the Scene list and clicking ADD NEW. Name the scene SphereScene. Move the 3D cursor to the left and add a UV Sphere, with the default settings of 32 rings and 32 segments (Space - Add - Mesh - UVSphere).

4) Save this blend file. Call it SourceFile.blend.

5) Now let's see how to get stuff from that file. Start by going to the default Blender setup. Select File - Load Factory Settings, and accept Erase All. We're going to get rid of everything, not just the default cube, but the lamp and the camera as well. To do this, press the Home key, which shows all the objects. With the default cube highlighted, press the SHIFT key and right click on the lamp. Then press the SHIFT key and right click on the camera. Press the DEL key and accept the defaults, deleting all the objects. We now have a blank scene, with no objects.

6) To see what objects we can import, go to File - Append or Link, or press SHIFT+ALT+F1. Select Object. All the objects in the SourceFile blend file are listed. Select Suzanne. Then click Load Library. Suzanne is appended to the new file. Append is the default mode. Note that she is green because she was green in the source file.

We can change Suzanne's color. With Suzanne highlighted, press the shading buttons (F5) and change her color to red by settng R=1, G=0, and B=0. However, if we press F12 to render, we get the error message "No Camera". That's because we don't have a camera, or a lamp for that matter.

So let's append the lamp and the camera as well. We can append more than one object at a time. Select File - Append or Link. Select the SourceScene. Instead of left clicking, hold the SHIFT key and right click on the camera. Then hold the SHIFT key down and right click on the lamp. The lamp and camera text should be highlighted. Click the Load Library button. The camera (named Camera) and lamp (named Spot) are now appended to the file. Press F12 to render. The monkey now renders properly.

7) Let's see how Link differs from Append. Select File - Append or Link, selecting the SourceScene again. Select the Cube (right click). Before loading the cube into the blend file, click the Link button. This will create a link to the cube. Click the Load Library button. The cube is linked into the file. Now let's try to change the cube's color by going to the Shading buttons. Guess what! We cannot do it! We get the message that we cannot edit external libdata.

_____

Link differs from Append in that while Append gives us a copy of the object and lets us change it, Link points back to the source object. By the way, not only can the color can't be changed, but any aspect of the data cannot be changed. A linked object can only be changed at the source. You cannot move it, rotate it, or scale it.

You might use Append to make a copy of an object but to be able to change it in the new blend file. Link is a better choice if you don't want anyone to change the object, such as a building that will have the same characteristics from one file to another.

8) Other things can be appended, such as materials. Let's load the factory settings again to start with the default Blender setup. Select the default cube and press F5 to go to the Shading buttons. Suppose we want to use the green material in the SourceFile. Instead of setting the sliders, we can select File - Append or Link and select SourceFile.blend. Select Material. Choose LightGreen, and click the LoadLibrary button. Now if we click the Materials, we see that LightGreen has been appended. The "O" before it means that there is no object that has that color, i.e. that LightGreen is an "orphan". If we click on it, however, the light green material is assigned to the cube. Now that the light green material has been assigned, the original material (called Material) has the "orphan" designation. An orphan material will be deleted when the file is saved. If you want to keep that material in the file, you need to create a Fake user by pressing the "F" button. You can create a blend file with your favorite materials, to use as a library, and append them as you need them.

9) You can append or link entire scenes. To illustrate, select our source file, choose Scene, and append the SphereScene by clicking on Load Library. The SphereScene is now available. Many other things, such as groups, meshes, and text objects, can be appended or linked.

Using append and link can save you hours of time and allow you to collaborate Blender development with others. You can split the workload and append or link each piece into the final product. I hope this gives you some ideas about how to use this powerful Blender feature. Happy Blendering!

Camera Fly Mode (2.49)

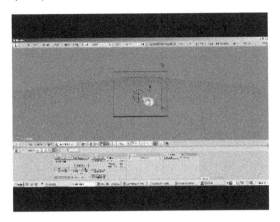

Watch the Video at: http://www.youtube.com/watch?v=M6DHd37qnnw

You may be familiar with the 3D View pan keys, CTRL+NUM2, CTRL+NUM4, CTRL+NUM6, and CTRL+NUM8, as well as NUM2, NUM4, NUM6, and NUM8, which let you rotate the view in small steps. You can, of course, also use the middle mouse button, or ALT+NUM1, to move around in the viewport. You may not be as familiar with Camera Fly Mode, which lets you fly around the 3D View, somewhat like a flight simulator. It's like you're in the cockpit of a jet plane, and you can navigate around. We're going to get into the cockpit, so to speak, to learn the controls. After that, I'll show you how you can use Camera Fly Mode to see the world through the eyes of, say, a character in your scene. You can move your character around to where you want it to be positioned.

So let's put our goggles on and get started. Start up Blender. We'll keep the default cube. Add Suzanne to the scene (Space - Add - Mesh - Monkey). Eventually, we'll get inside her head.

Now start your engines. Press SHIFT+F, which gets you into Camera Fly Mode. You see the corners of a rectangle. This is sort of like the navigator's view. Think of the mouse as a joy stick. Move the mouse upward. The view is panned upward. The further away the mouse gets from the rectangle, the more pronounced the panning. Now move the moust downward. The view is panned downward, back towards the monkey and the rectangle. Move the mouse back inside the rectangle. The panning stops. As long as the cursor is inside the rectangle, there is no panning. Now move the mouse to the right. The view rotates counterclockwise. Move the mouse back to the left, inside te cursor. The rotation stops. Move the mouse to the left. The view

rotates clockwise. Move the mouse to the right, to back inside the
rectangle. The rotation stops.

You can also use the mouse wheel, or if you don't have a mouse wheel,
the plus and minus keys on the numeric keypad, to pan inward and
outward. I'll assume that you don't have a mouse wheel - not
everyone does. We'll use the plus and minus keys on the numeric
keypad. Press the minus key on the numeric keypad to pan outward.
To stop this, press the plus key on the numeric keypad. To reverse
direction, panning inward, press the plus key on the numeric keypad.
To stop that, press the minus key on the numeric keypad.

When you're finished panning and rotating, you have one of two
options. Maybe you like where you wound up. If you did, left click,
the view stays there. On the other hand, you might want to return
back to where you started, to fly home, so to speak. If you prefer
that, press Esc.

So that's Camera Fly mode in a nutshell. Here's a little trick that
might come in handy. We're going to get inside Suzanne's head, and
fly with her. I think biologists do this sort of thing with
migrating birds or fish to see where they go. In the process, we can
move Suzanne to where she has the best view of the scene. To do
this, first press the Z key to go into wireframe mode. Then select
Suzanne. Now make Suzanne the "active camera" by either pressing
CTRL+Num0 or from the View menu, select Cameras, then Select Active
Object as Active Camera. Now you see the world from Suzanne's point
of view, so to speak. Press SHIFT+F to go into Camera Fly mode. You
can move Suzanne around using all the controls we used earlier. If
you like where she ends up, left mouse click to move her there.
Press the Home key, which shows all the objects in the scene, to see
where she wound up.

Eventually, you want to make the real camera the active camera. To
do that, press ALT+Num0, or from the View Menu, select Cameras, and
then Camera.

Grease Pencil Tricks (2.49)

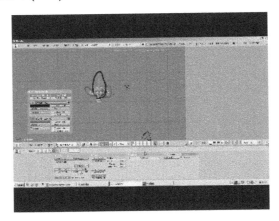

Watch the Video at: http://www.youtube.com/watch?v=ovhIniLYuM0

The Grease Pencil is a relatively recent addition to Blender, introduced in version 2.48. The Grease Pencil at first glance looks like something out of a primitive Paint program, and in fact it operates similarly to pencil tools in 2D image programs like the Gimp and Photoshop. What is such an apparently primitive tool doing in a sophisticated 3D modeling program like Blender? It seems so out of place. Was someone bored one day and decided to create a tool that creates doodles? Actually, the grease pencil originated from the early days of animation, where animators used an actual pencil (remember that?) to sketch out an animation. Blender's grease pencil can do this as well. As it turns out, the Grease Pencil actually has a lot of useful features. The purpose of this video is to suggest some of them.

So let's start up Blender with the default cube. We'll ignore the cube and just concentrate on the grease pencil. To access the Grease Pencil, go to the View Menu, selecting the Grease Pencil option. Click the Use Grease Pencil button. Here's a little gotcha. If you start drawing on the view, instead of drawing, Blender rotates the cube! That's because the Grease Pencil requires a drawing layer, which is not turned on by default. Blender's hinting system interprets your attempts at drawing as a hint that you want the cube to be rotated. Blender is only trying to be helpful. However, that is not what we want here.

So press ESC. Blender's Grease Pencil needs a layer to draw on. If you have ever used a 2D image editing program like the Gimp or Photoshop, the layer concept is very similar. Click the Draw Mode button. As soon as you do that, you can start drawing on the 3D window. You draw by left clicking the mouse and dragging. Automatically, a Layer called GP_Layer is created, with a black pencil. The pencil may appear to be drawing directly on the 3D window, but actually it is drawing on the layer.

Here are some basic grease pencil features. Draw a non-straight line by holding the left mouse button and dragging. Stop the line drawing by releasing the left mouse button.

Place the 3D cursor at another place in the 3D viewport. To draw a straight line, hold the control key as well as the left mouse button, and drag. At first, even if you go off course, the line appears to be curved. However, when you finish drawing the line, by releasing the left mouse button, the line becomes straight.

To erase an area, hold down the Alt Key and the right mouse button, and drag. You can also erase stroke by stroke. Add a line. To erase it, click the Erase Last Stroke button.

You can change the color by clicking on the color rectangle and choosing a new color as you would choose a color anywhere else in Blender. Let's draw some lines and change their color to red. The color affects the entire layer. You cannot change the color on only part of the layer. However, you can create a new layer and change its color. To do this, click the Add New Layer button. A new layer dialog displays. The layers are stacked, in a similar way to the Gimp or Photoshop. Change the color of this layer to blue. In addition to the color, you can change the pencil's thickness. Increase the thickness to 1, and make some thick blue lines.

Add a green layer, increase the thickness, and add a few green lines. Now we have 3 layers. As with the Gimp or Photoshop, we can change the active layer by clicking on it. Click on the blue layer to highlight it. Add a line. The line is added on the blue layer. We can also hide layers by clicking on the eye icon. Click on the eye to hide the blue layer. Only the red and green layers display, and the blue layer is marked as hidden. To make the blue layer visible, click the eye icon again.

Let's look at opacity, an area where the grease pencil works slightly different from an image editor. Turn the opacity of the blue layer up fully to 1. The layer is fully opaque, which is how image editor layers work as well. However, if you turn the opacity to zero, there's still a ghost outline of the original lines on the layer. Even turning the opacity to zero in all the layers leaves ghostly outlines of the drawings. In an image editor, the drawings would disappear. If you want a layer not to draw, just hide it.

You can draw in 3D space. To activate that, click the Sketch in 3D button. Rotate the view by using the middle mouse button. Draw lines as you go. The lines are drawn in a third dimension.

OK, great, you might say. So we can doodle on our model. Big deal. Can we do anything useful with the grease pencil other than waste some time.

Sure. Here's one idea. The grease pencil also works in the UV/Image editor. To illustrate this, split the 3D window. Change the window type to UV/Image Editor. Click on Draw Mode. Draw a happy face. You can actually freehand draw directly on the UV/Image Edtor this way. If you want your doodle to be added to the image, click the Stick To View button.

Here's another. Suppose you're part of a team that is building a new monkey character which is based on Suzanne but with a somewhat different look. Let's start with the default Blender scene, by selecting Load Factory Settings from the File menu. Delete the default cube (right click, then X to confirm the delete). Add the monkey mesh (Space - Add - Mesh - Monkey). Get rid of the 3D Transform Manipulator. From the View Menu, select Grease Pencil. Click the Use Grease Pencil button. Then click the Draw Mode button. Maybe you want her head to be more egg shaped. So draw an egg shaped head in black.

Your teammate wants to change the monkey's ears to look more like Spock's. You attach the blend file with your suggestion. Your colleague can use the Grease Pencil tool, add a new layer, change the color to red, and sketch the pointy ears. Split the 3D viewport and make the right window a Text window. Add a new text area and add comments. This way, both suggestions are noted.

Another powerful feature is that grease pencil notations can be converted to a mesh, as the start of a model. To do that, select the layer with the new ears and click the Convert to button. Convert the ear sketch to a Bezier curve. Turn off the Grease Pencil tool. With the new ear-Bezier curve selected, press ALT+C. You can convert the ear to a mesh and start modeling.

You can annotate an animation with the grease pencil. To illustrate this, start with the default Blender scene by selecting Load Factory Settings from the File menu. Get rid of the 3D Transform Manipulator. Go to the SR-1:Animation layout. From the View Menu, select Grease Pencil. Click the Use Grease Pencil button. Then click the Draw Mode button. Draw a black line. It's actually drawn on a layer associated with Frame 1. Go to Frame 21. Draw another

black line. If you scrub the animation, by dragging the green line
in the IPO curve editor, you'll see the line on Frame 1 change to the
other line on Frame 21. You can prototype how the animation looks in
this way.

I hope this gives you some ideas for using the grease pencil
productively.

Mesh Modeling

Pivot Points (2.5)

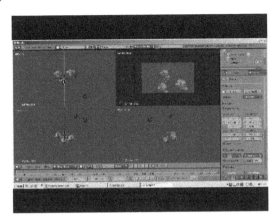

Watch the Video at: http://www.youtube.com/watch?v=HsACGGeym2o

The goal of this video is to get you comfortable moving around in
Blender 2.5. If you're going to continue with Blender, 2.5 will be
your new home. The developers just made 2.5 the official "trunk" for
Blender development. That means that future development will be
exclusively in 2.5. Work on older versions will, most likely, be
limited to bug fixes and, as 2.5 becomes the standard.

Scaling and rotating objects are a fundamental Blender skill. The
pivot point defines how objects will be rotated and scaled. If
you're relatively new to Blender, you can easily get objects moving
in ways you might not expect. As we progress, I will point out
differences between Blender 2.5 and the older versions. The pivoting
actions really haven't changed in 2.5. However, some cosmetic things
like the default color of the active object and the icons for
rotation and scaling, have changed. You should feel very comfortable
pivoting your way in 2.5 almost immediately.

We start with the default Blender scene. First, we delete the
default cube. Before, you could either use the DEL key or press X.
In 2.5, only X works. The DEL key does nothing. So press X and
confirm the delete.

We'll add the monkey object, by pressing the SPACE bar. Something
happens, but it's not what you expect. You get a different menu than

before, a menu that has nothing to do with adding objects. Press ESC. We'll save discussion of that menu for another time. Instead, press SHIFT+A, which is the keyboard shortcut for adding objects. SHIFT+A brings up the familiar object add menu. Select Add-Mesh-Monkey, as before.

Let's look at the outliner window, in the upper right corner of the screen, and scroll down. Guess what? Suzanne isn't there. She has been renamed "Mesh". I guess they'll have to rename the Suzanne Award.

We'll create 3 monkey objects to demonstrate rotation. First, duplicate our monkey - it will take a bit of time getting used to the name "Mesh" - with SHIFT+D. SHIFT+D works as before. We grab the copy and move it away from the original, and left click to confirm. Then we press SHIFT+D to create another copy and drag it to form a triangle of monkeys.

Switch to Quad View, a new built in view, by going to the View menu, and selecting Toggle Quad View. The window is divided into 4 windows, Top, Front, Right, and Camera, that make it, in my opinion, much easier to navigate around your scene than before. Since Toggle Quad View is a toggle, by selecting Toggle Quad View again, you get back to the startup scene, with just one 3D window.

We'll work in Quad View. Adjust the monkeys positions so that they look right in Top View and Camera View. We'll work in Top View. Select the first monkey with right click. Then hold down the SHIFT key, Right Click, and select the second monkey. Hold down the SHIFT key, Right click, and select the third monkey. Note that the default color for the selected object and the active object - the last one you selected, and the name that displays in the lower left hand corner - has changed from pink to orange. I think orange is much easier to see. The active object has a light orange border, as opposed the light pink in the older Blender versions.

The default pivot mode is Bounding Box center, which means that the pivot point is defined by the bounding box. The Move Object Centers Only is off by default, as before. Press the R key to rotate the monkeys. Note that the rotation icon is double arrows, and that the monkeys rotate around the bounding box center. Pressing Escape cancels the rotation, as before.

Just for fun, press the R key twice (R and R). This allows you to rotate in 3 dimensions. It's a neat feature and not very well known. Press ESC to cancel.

Turn the Move Object Centers button on. This makes rotation and scaling affect the object center only, not the objects themselves.

Now press the R key and rotate. The monkeys do not tilt as they rotate. Press ESC to cancel the rotation, and turn off the Move Object Centers Only button.

Now press S to scale. With the Move Object Centers Only button inactive, all the monkeys grow or shrink. Press ESC to cancel the scaling. Now turn on the Move Object Centers Only button and press the S key. Now, the monkeys don't grow or shrink, BUT they do get nearer or farther away from each other while preserving their relative position. This is useful for repositioning objects in your scene. Press ESC and turn off the Move Object Centers Only button.

Now open the Pivot Menu and select Active Object as your pivot point. Press R to rotate. Now the monkeys tilt while they rotate around the active object, similar to the bounding box behavior. Press ESC to cancel.

Turn on the Move Object Centers Only button and press the R key. Now the monkeys keep facing forward as they rotate around the active object. Press ESC to cancel the rotation, and turn off Move Object Centers Only.

Press the S key to scale. The monkeys grow and shrink. Press ESC to cancel the scaling. Turn on the Move Object Centers Only button and press the S key. Now the monkeys move away from or closer to each other but do not grow or shrink. Press ESC to cancel. Turn off the Move Object Centers Only button.

Open up the Pivot Menu and select Individual Centers as your pivot point. Press R to rotate. Each monkey rotates around its center point. Press ESC and turn on the Move Object Centers button. Now when you press R to rotate, nothing happens. That's because only the centers (all 3 of them) rotate. The monkeys don't do anything. Press ESC to cancel.

Turn off the Move Object Centers button and press S to scale. Now the monkeys grow and shrink in unison, like a dance line. Press ESC to cancel and turn on the Move Object Centers button. Again, the monkeys don't do anything because only the centers scale, and each of them is only a point to begin with. Press ESC to cancel and turn off the Move Object Centers button.

Open up the Pivot Menu and select 3D Cursor as your pivot point. The behavior of rotation and scaling is the same as for Bounding Box and Active Object, except that the pivot is around wherever the 3D cursor is situated.

Our final pivot point type, Median Point, is the center point for all the selected objects. This is similar to Bounding Box center, except that the median point might be, and usually is, different from the bounding box center because objects tend to have different sizes. As you see, the behavior is similar, but the pivot point is slightly different.

To summarize, pivoting is basically the same as before. However, because of the new Quad View, the better choice of colors and icons, and the improved design of the startup screen, it's much easier to see what's going on.

Object Origin (Center) (2.5)

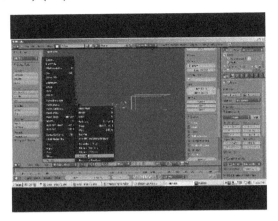

Watch the Video at: http://www.youtube.com/watch?v=wmCRTfa8YJk

Each object in Blender has a center point. In 2.5, this is called
the Object Origin. In Blender 2.49 the origin was called the Object
Center, although the problem is that the object's origin is not
always at the center, and this can cause problems.

Add a monkey (SHIFT+A - Mesh - Monkey). Move the monkey (G key) so
that the monkey displays separately from the cube. Select the cube
object. Make sure the cube is in Object Mode. If it's not, press
the tab key. Turn off the translate manipulator widget. Zoom in a
bit. The cube's center point, or origin, is the small dot in center
of cube. By default it's not visible unless the object is selected.
To see all the object origins, whether or not the object is selected,
press the N key to bring up the properties panel of the 3D viewport.
Check the Display All Object Origins check box. If the check box is
not selected, only the object origin of the selected object displays.

Press the Z key to go to wireframe mode. Here is the object origin.
Turn on the translate manipulator widget. The widget is located at
the object origin when the object is selected. You can move the cube
along the X axis (red), the Y axis (green), or the Z axis (blue)
using the translate manipulator.

Hold the SHIFT key down and click on the rotate manipulator widget.
This adds the rotate manipulator to the translate manipulator. The
rotate manipulator is also located at object origin. The object
rotates relative to the position of the object origin, along the X,
Y, or Z axis.

Hold the SHIFT key down and click on the scale manipulator widget. This adds the scale manipulator widget, which is also located at object origin. The object scales relative to the X, Y, or Z axis.

Switch back to translate manipulator widget.

Tab into Edit mode. Deselect all the vertices by pressing the A key. Go to Front View (NUM1). Box select all the vertices, move them to the right. Object origin is now not in center of object. This is what happens when you manipulate object subcomponents in edit mode. Select all the vertices and move them all, in edit mode. Tab into Object Mode.

Now the object origin not even inside the object.

There is no method to select the object origin. However, there is a command to move the origin to the center of object. From the Object menu, select Transform, then Origin to Geometry. This commanbd moves the object's origin point to the center of object geometry. The shortcut is SHIFT+CTRL+Alt+C.

In 2.49 this command was called Center New and was activated by pressing a button. It's good modeling practice to set the object's origin to the center of the object.

You can create a tool button to set the origin, similar to Center, Center New, and Center Cursor in 2.49. Click the Add Tool button. Type in Set Origin. Select Set Origin from list. Now there's a tool button to set the object's origin. Then tab to edit mode, leaving the origin point behind. Set origin tool button, now setting Origin to Geometry. Now the origin is at the center of the object.

To summarize, making sure that the origin point of your object is where you want it to be, usually at the object's center, can prevent you from getting unexpected results when you're modeling.

Separating Objects (2.5)

Watch the Video at: http://www.youtube.com/watch?v=IRvrBmHaE4k

Thank you to Neal Hirsig (nhirsig@tufts.edu) on which this video is based. His video is at http://www.gryllus.net. Blender lets you separate subcomponents of an object, creating a new data block, creating a separate object.

Start with the default Blender scene. Go to the Outliner editor window. Drag the bottom border of the outliner window down to show all the objects. In the Properties window, click on the Object icon, which looks like a cube. Rename the Cube object to Box. Note that the new name displays in the outliner as well. Select the box object and tab into edit mode. Select the top four vertices of the box. Press the P key, which displays Separate dialog box. You can separate by Selection, Material, or Loose Parts (unconnected subcomponents). Separate by Selection. The top part of the box is now its own object.

Tab out of Edit mode and select the separated object. In the Object window, rename the object Box Lid. Scale the lid up a slight bit. Tab into Edit mode, deselect the vertices (A key). Press CTRL+TAB and go into Edge Selection mode. Select the 4 edges, extrude them down a bit, in the -Z direction, forming the box lid.

Then tab out of Edit mode. From Object menu, select Transform, then select Origin to Center of Geometry. Then press the G key, then the Z key to constrain the movement to the Z axis, and place the box lid on top of the box. This separates and places the box lid on top of the box. Often it is necessary to create a separate object from parts of another object.

Loops (2.49)

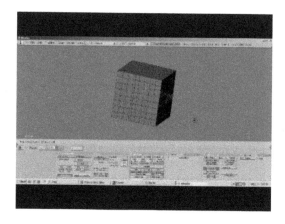

Watch the Video at: http://www.youtube.com/watch?v=Nj15p716qDs

You can select the subcomponents of a mesh by either RMB, or SHIFT+RMB, or the B key to box select, or the B key twice to form a circle selection, or ALT+LMB for lasso select. There's another way to select parts of a mesh, which is by selecting a loop of vertices, edges, or faces. Also, adding loops is a great way to add detail to your mesh. Instead of subdividing a mesh, which adds a lot of extra geometry when it's not needed, adding loops only in the area where you want detail will create a cleaner mesh with fewer edges, vertices, and faces. The aim of this tutorial is to demonstrate how to use loops both to select parts of your mesh and to add details to it.

We'll work with the default cube. It's selected and in Object Mode. Go to the Edit buttons (F9) and press Tab to go into Edit mode. Press the Subdivide button, in the Mesh Tools panel, three times. Rotate the view, using either the middle mouse button or ALT+NUM1 if you enabled Emulate 3 Button Mouse in the Preferences window. We're in Vertex Select mode. Position the 3D Cursor at one of the corner vertices. Hold the Alt key down and press the Right Mouse button. Doing that, selects not just the vertex (which is what Right Mouse button does just by itself), but the entire edge that the vertex belongs to. Press the A key to deselect the vertices.

Now hold the ALT key down and select a vertex that is not on the outside edge but instead is inside the cube. This time, an entire loop of edges is selected - the loop that that vertex belongs to. The loop could be horizontal or vertical.

Press the A key to deselect everything. You can also select the perpendicular range of faces to which the edge belongs by holding both the CTRL key and the ALT key at the same time. To illustrate, press the CTRL key and the ALT key at the same time, and select a vertex. What is selected is the faces on the edge perpendicular to the vertex.

You can add to the loop selection, in effect selecting multiple loops, by holding the SHIFT Key down as well as the ALT Key. Hold the both the Alt and SHIFT keys and select an unselected vertex. Now you have selected two loops. If the loop includes all the vertices that form a face, those faces will be selected as well.

If you feel particularly ambidextrous, try holding the CTRL, ALT, and SHIFT keys down at the same time, and select another vertex. You then add to the faces selected before.

Loop selection works in edge select mode as well. Holding the Alt key and then clicking the right mouse button selects the loop to which the edge belongs to. Press the A key to deselect everything. If we go into Face Select mode, we see that loops of faces can also be selected this way. Hold the Alt key, and with the 3D cursor on a face, press the right mouse button to select a face loop. Hold both the SHIFT key and the ALT key, select an unselected face with the right mouse button, and the loop in which the selected face belongs is added to the selection. Selecting loops of vertices, edges, or faces, can make the selection process much more precise than box selection or selection of individual vertices, edges, or faces.

You can add edge loops with the Loop Subdivide tool (CTRL+R). To illustrate, position the cursor on an edge of the cube, and press CTRL+R. A magenta square shows where the new loop will be cut. However, you actually have more control over where the loop cut will occur. Press Enter. Now you see both the proposed new loop, and a green line, which is the edge along which you can slide this loop. This is called "edge slide mode". A green line, showing the edge along which the loop can be cut, displays. You can scroll the edge up and down along the green line. Press Enter when you get to the position of the new edge that you want.

You can create more than one edge loop at a time. Position the cursor at an edge along where you would like to cut and press CTRL+R. Now, instead of pressing Enter, press the + key on the numeric keypad. This adds a loop cut, allowing you to create two loop cuts at a time. You can press the + key on the numeric keypad to add another loop cut, or you can press the - key on the numeric keypad to subtract 1 loop cut. Then press Enter. Edge Slide mode does not work when you create more than one edge loop. Instead, the loops are split evenly along the edge.

Let's start with the default scene by selecting Load Factory Settings from the menu. Delete the default cube (press the DEL key, then press OK to accept the delete). Add a UV Sphere (Space - Add - Mesh - UVSphere), accepting the default settings of 32 rings and 32 segments. Press Tab to go into Edit Mode. Press A to deselect everything. Press CTRL+R. You can create edge loops either based on rings (going left and right) or segments (going up and down). Lets add an edge loop based on a ring. Press CTRL+R, selecting a horizontal edge loop to create. This selection works the same way as for a cube. Press Enter, to go into Edge Slide mode. Position the loop where you want and press Enter. However, for a ring, the edge loop only is created on half the UV Sphere. Press CTRL+R, then Enter. Slide the edge where you want it. Then press Enter. Rotate the UV Sphere and you will see the result. To get the edge loop to go around the UV Sphere, you will need to create the corresponding edge loop on the other side of the sphere.

You can add more than one loop cut using the + key on the numeric keypad, and subtract using the - key on the numeric keypad, as with the cube.

CTRL+ALT+RMB and SHIFT+CTRL+ALT+RMB work the same way on a UV Sphere as on a cube. You can create a loop of faces perpendicular to the edge you select with CTRL+ALT+RMB, and extend the selection if you somehow manage to hold Shift, Control, Alt, and Right Click while the 3D cursor is on an unselected face.

As you can see, selecting and adding loops can make your mesh modeling more precise when you're adding detail. These techniques work on any mesh, not just the cube or UV Sphere. Try them with a torus, or with Suzanne, and you should get the hang of loop selection and addition quickly.

Empty Object (2.5)

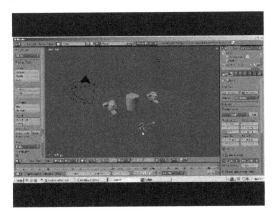

Watch the Video at: http://www.youtube.com/watch?v=eJ4qTOAN2V4

A big thank you to Neal Hirsig (nhirsig@tufts.edu), who created the
tutorial on which this tutorial is based, at http://www.gryllus.net.
An Empty Object is a non renderable object that represents a point in
space.

Start with the Blender default scene. Delete the default cube by
pressing the E key and confirming the delete. Add a Tube object
(SHIFT+A - Mesh - Tube). Add a Monkey object (SHIFT+A - Mesh -
Monkey). Move it along the Y axis by pressing the G key, then the Y
key, and dragging the monkey. Duplicate the monkey (SHIFT+D) and
move the duplicated monkey to the other side of the tube object, by
pressing the G key, then the Y key, then dragging. To add an Empty
Object press SHIFT+A and then select Empty from the Add menu. Move
the Empty object down a bit.

An Empty Object is represented as an axis icon. Turn of the
Transform Widget to see this better. Press the N key to bring up the
Properties panel of the 3D Viewport. Although it is non renderable,
an Empty Object has a location, rotation, and scale. Press the N key
to hide the Properties panel of the 3D Viewport. An empty object is
often used as a placeholder or a proxy object. In most cases it is
used as a parent to other objects.

Select the monkey on the left. Then SHIFT+RMB to add the tube to the
selection. Press SHIFT+RMB to add the monkey on the right to the
selection. Press SHIFT+RMB to add the Empty object to the selection.
Press CTRL+P to make the Empty the parent of the other three objects.
Now we can select the Empty Object, press the G key, and move the

three objects by moving just the Empty Object. Undo the parenting of the Empty Object by pressing ALT+P and selecting Clear Parent.

An Empty Object is also sometimes used as a reference point. Select the Tube object. Tab into Edit mode. Deselect the vertices with the A key. Select the center vertex at the bottom of the tube. You can reference the center vertex on bottom of the tube multiple times during modeling. Press SHIFT+S and snap the cursor to the selected vertex. Tab out of Edit mode. Add an empty object with SHIFT+A to reference the vertex. Now you can use the second Empty object to snap the cursor to the vertex, instead of having to go into Edit mode again to select the vertex.

An Empty Object is often used as part of a constraint system. We'll make the first Empty Object as the target of the constraint. Select the Camera object. Add a Track To constraint. To: = -Z and Up: Y. Make the first Empty object (Empty) the Target of the constraint. The camera is now tracking the Empty object. If the camera is moved, it still points to the empty object. This is a convenient method of animating or focusing the camera or what the camera is focused on. Moving the Empty object makes the camera move as well.

Empty objects can be duplicated.   One Empty Object can be the parent of another Empty Object. You'll discover many uses of the Empty Object as you grow and develop your Blender modeling skills.

Array Modifier (2.5)

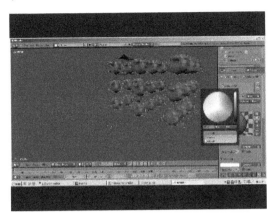

Watch the Video at: http://www.youtube.com/watch?v=y3oSgZEdsmc

The purpose of this video is both to make you comfortable with the user interface of Blender 2.5 and to show how Blender's array modifier works. The array modifier is a handy way of creating a lot of objects quickly. It's much more efficient than duplicating each object with SHIFT+D and then positioning it. Our goal is to create a "cube array" of 27 monkeys, 3 in the X direction, 3 in the Y direction, and 3 in the Z direction. You could easily create an army of hundreds, or even thousands, of objects, in a few keystrokes. If you're creating a game with thousands of aliens, the array modifier will save you many hours duplicating all those characters.

Even though I created this video with a mid-September pre alpha build of Blender 2.5, which means that everything is subject to change before the final version of Blender 2.5 is released, the array modifier works the same way as in Blender 2.4x versions. So let's get started.

Start up Blender 2.5, with its default scene. Delete the default cube, which is selected by default. If it's not, right click to select. Use the X key (the DEL key doesn't work) and confirm the delete.

We'll start with one monkey. Add the monkey to the scene by pressing SHIFT+A (the space bar gives you a different menu), then Add-Mesh-Monkey. Click on the Modifier panel, an icon that looks like a wrench, and click on Add Modifier. Click on Array. You will see two monkeys. The default is a fixed count array, where you specify the number of objects in the array, set to 2 objects, with a relative offset X of 1 Blender Unit, with Y and Z offsets of 0. The numbers you see in the relative offset and the constant offset X, Y, and Z areas are in Blender Units. You can use either Relative Offset, Constant Offset, or both, to position the array objects.

Constant Offset tells Blender to position the duplicate copy the number of Blender Units in the X, Y, or Z direction, from the center of the previous object. Relative Offset uses the actual width of the object, in the X, Y, or Z direction. In the perspective view, you can see how you can control the positioning of the monkeys in the up and down, left and right, or side to side, using either Relative Offset, Constant Offset, or both.

Instead of Fixed Count, you can use Fit Length. When you choose Fit Length, the Array Modifier will add as many monkeys as will fit in the number of Blender Units specified. The offset settings, constant or relative, need to be taken into account to determine how many monkeys fit. If you increase the spacing between the monkeys, you will reduce the number of monkeys in the array.

Another option is Fit Curve. You control the number of copies by creating a curve and increasing or decreasing its length. Any one of Blender's curve objects - Bezier curve, Bezier circle, NURBS curve, NURBS circle, or Path - will work. Mesh objects will not work. We'll create a Bezier curve as an example. You need to tell the Array Modifier the name of the curve. The default name is Curve, which we enter in the Object box. The name is case sensitive. As soon as we do that, the curve will control the number of monkeys generated. This is a great way to animate duplicate copies because the curve can be animated.

Delete the curve, by right clicking on it, pressing X, and confirming the delete.

Go back to Fixed Count. We'll now create our 27 monkeys arrayed in a cube fashion. Start off by creating 3 monkeys in the X direction, with the X offset of 1.5, to give us some space between the monkeys. Press Apply, which makes the change to the object permanent. We now have cloned 3 monkeys in the X direction.

Next we clone the 3 monkeys 3 times in the Y direction. Click on Add Modifier and select Array. This time, the X offset will be 0, and the Y offset will be 1.5, which gives space in the Y direction. Press Apply. Now we have 9 monkeys in a 3 x 3 grid.

Finally, we clone the nine monkeys 3 times in the Z direction. Click on Add Modifier. Select Array. Set the X offset to 0, the Y offset to 0, and the Z offset to 1.5. The result is 27 monkeys in a cube style arrangement.

The monkey array is actually one object. To illustrate that, let's make them all red. Click the Material button and set the diffuse color to Red by using the slider.

I'll switch to Quad View to illustrate how we can see the front, side, top, and camera views of our monkey cube, all at once.

The array modifier is a flexible and quick way to clone objects in Blender.

Snap Tools (2.49)

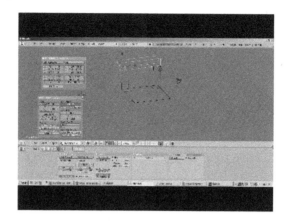

Watch the Video at: http://www.youtube.com/watch?v=1LUez1HPUf4

One of the most important skills in Blender mesh modeling is the
ability to position objects precisely. This is especially true in
architectural models, where you are closely following a blueprint, or
in a product model, where you need to position a part, such as the
tires or doors on a car, exactly. If your mesh is complicated, it
can be a difficult task because of the many vertices or faces that
are close together.

Blender provides a number of tools that make it much easier to
position objects more exactly. A commonly used tool is the Snap Menu
which will be the subject of this tutorial which, combined with an
understanding of how the 3D cursor and the transform widget work,
should help a lot. I want to make the explanation simple because
this topic often confuses beginning Blender users. I know because at
my forum, at http://forum.irakrakow.com, and in emails, I have been
asked these type of object positioning questions many times. We'll
use as an example the common task of positioning columns precisely
above and across a ground plane. I used Blender Version 2.49b.

Start with the default scene. We'll keep the default cube and first,
go into Front View (NUM1). You can tell if you're in Front View if
the blue arrow (the Z axis) is pointing upward. Add a plane (Space -
Add - Mesh - Plane). Press the Z key to go into wireframe mode.
That way, we see the geometry better. Select the cube. We'll scale
the cube a bit so that it looks like a column. To do that, pres the
S key, then the Z key, then 3, then Enter, to scale the cube up 3
times in the Z direction.

Scale the plane up 5 times (Right Click to select, then S, 5, and Enter). Zoom out 3 or 4 times, using the NUM- key. Panning with the middle mouse button (or ALT+NUM1 if you have selected the Emulate 3 Button Mouse button in the Preferences Menu) shows that the cube, the basis for our column, is half above the plane and half below it. Don't worry. We'll fix this.

Our first job is to snap the column to the top left corner of the ground plane. First, let's locate the 3D cursor and the transform widget. Left click anywhere a few times in the 3D window. The 3D cursor is the circular icon, with a cross, that follows where you click. You can find out where the 3D cursor is by clicking on View Properties from the View Menu. Note how the X, Y, and Z coordinates of the 3D cursor change as you click in different areas of the 3D window.

Where the selected object is, is another matter entirely. Select the cube. Press the N key to bring up the Transform Properties window. The LocX, LocY, and LocZ coordinates show the center of either the selected object or objects. Right now, the cube is centered at 0,0,0, as is the plane.

Moving the column around to try to get it to align to the top left corner of the plane by just grabbing it with the G key is difficult. Here's a way to get an exact snap. First, select the column cube. Tab into Edit mode. Right click on the bottom left vertex to select it. Note that while the 3D cursor hasn't changed its position, the Transform Properties window is telling us that the selection is at the vertex with X=-1, Y=1, and Z=-1. The Transform Widget has moved to that position as well.

We're going to use the Snap Menu to position the column exactly. Press SHIFT+S to bring up the Snap Menu. The menu has options which either move the Selection, or move the 3D cursor. We're going to reposition the 3D cursor at the Selection. Select Cursor -> Selection. This moves the 3D cursor to the Selection. Now the 3D Cursor is in the exact position as the vertex we selected (X=-1, Y=1, and Z=-3). If that's true, how come the VertexX, VertexY, and VertexZ coordinates are different? That's because the coordinates are different. Click the Global button in the Transform Properties window. Now the coordinates match. The original vertex position was in local coordinates, positioned relative to the object's center.

The next step is to Tab out of Edit mode. In the Mesh Tools panel there are a series of buttons related to changing the center of selected objects. Right now, the column's object center is 0,0,0. We want it to be at the selected vertex (-1, 1, -3). To do that go to the Edit buttons (F9) and click Center Cursor. Now the transform widget, showing the center of the post is exactly at the selected vertex.

Next, select the ground plane. Press SHIFT+S and select Cursor -> Selection. In the Transform Properties window, note that the Plane is selected and the cursor is at -5, 5, 0 in global coordinates. This is also the position of the cursor.

Tab out of Edit mode. Select the column. Press SHIFT+S again. This time, select Selection -> Cursor. The column snaps to the upper left corner of the ground plane.

Let's repeat this procedure to create a new column and snap it to the upper right vertex of the plane. First press SHIFT+D to create a duplicate of the column. Move the duplicated column a bit so we see it as an individual column. Tab into Edit Mode. Select the upper right vertex of the column. Press SHIFT+S to bring up the Snap menu, and select Cursor -> Selection. Tab into Object Mode. From the Edit buttons (F9), in Mesh Tools, click Center Cursor. Select the Plane. Tab into Edit Mode. Select the Plane's upper right vertex. Press SHIFT+S and select Cursor -> Selection. Tab out of Edit Mode. Select the Column. Press SHIFT+S. Select Selection -> Cursor. The column should snap in place.

Now for the fun part. How can we position a beam across the columns? First, go to Front View (NUM1). With a column select, press SHIFT+D to duplicate. Move the column a bit so we see it individually. Rotate the column on its side 90 degrees (R - 90 - Enter). Tab into Edit Mode. Select the lower left vertex of the cube. From the Edit buttons, click the Center Cursor button. Select the original column. Tab into Edit mode. Select the upper left vertex of the column. Press SHIFT+S to bring up the Snap menu. Select Cursor -> Selection. Tab out of Edit mode. Select the beam. Press SHIFT+S. Select Selection -> Cursor.

The beam doesn't extend to the end of the second column. This is easy to fix. Note that the dimensions of the beam are 2 x 2 x 6 Blender units. Select the plane. Note that its dimensions are 10 x 10. Reselect the beam. Change DimX to 10. Now the beam fits exactly on the two columns, for the dimension of the ground plane.

Rip Tool (2.49)

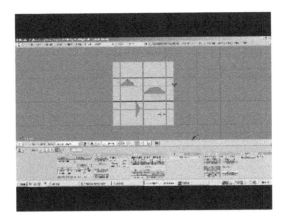

Watch the Video at: http://www.youtube.com/watch?v=XyMAMfd3-Sc

The Rip tool lets you tear out a hole, such as a mouth or an eye socket if you're modeling a face, in your mesh.   You can use the Rip Tool in either vertex select or edge select mode. The Rip Tool does not work in Face Select Mode. You can also use the Rip tool to do split apart a mesh, for example, splitting a sphere into two halves. You can create faces to join the parts of the mesh that you have ripped.   The goal of this tutorial is to make you comfortable both ripping a mesh apart to create holes where you want them, and to join mesh parts together again.

We'll start with the default Blender 2.49b scene.   Delete the default cube (press the DEL key and press Enter to confirm). Add a plane (Space - Add - Mesh - Plane). The plane is in Object mmode. Scale the plane to 4 times its original size (S - 4 - Enter). Get rid of the 3D Transform Manipulator to make the demonstration of the Rip Tool easier to follow.

Press Tab to go into Edit mode. Press the Edit buttons (F9) and click the Subdivide button 3 times. Press the A key to deselect all vertices.

Look at the indicators for vertices, edges, and faces. Right now, the plane has 81 vertices, 144 edges, and 64 faces. The zeroes show that nothing is selected.

Make sure you are in Vertex Select Mode (Control - Tab - 1) or the Vertex Select icon. Position the 3D cursor below and to the right of

the vertex you want to select. Select the vertex, then press the V
key, grabbing the vertex to the right. A hole is created to the
right of the vertex. Look at the indicators for vertices, edges, and
faces. Before the plane had 81 vertices, of which none were
selected. Now, the plane has 82 vertices, and one is selected.

This gives a clue as to what the Rip tool actually does. It creates
a duplicate vertex at the same spot as the selected vertex, connected
to the vertices as the copied vertex. When the mesh is ripped, that
vertex drags the adjacent edges with it. The 3D cursor position
determines the direction of the rip.

Press ALT+U, which brings up the Undo History. Click on Select to
undo the rip. Now we're back to having the vertex selected, with 81
vertices altgether. Move the cursor above and to the left of the
selected vertex. You can constrain the rip to an axis. To do that,
press the V key, and then the Y key to constrain the rip to the Y
axis. Press Enter to confirm. So you can see that the direction of
the rip depends on the position of the 3D cursor at the time that you
press the V key. The rip is along the edge that is closest to the
selected vertex.

Press the A key to deselect the vertex. Go to another part of the
plane, and select a vertex. Then Shift select (Shift - Right Click)
the vertex immediately to the right of it. Position the 3D cursor
above and in the middle of the selected vertices. Press the V key.
You now get a bigger rip, a trapezoid, with 2 vertices on top and 4
vertices on the bottom. So a rip with N selected vertices produces a
ripped polygon with N vertices in the ripped direction and N+2
vertices in the original direction.

If you start the Rip and then immediately decide not to continue, the
new vertices still remain. To illustrate this, select a vertex,
press the V key, and then press Esc. The vertex created by the Rip
tool is still there. You can rip the mesh now even though you
pressed Esc. Press the G key and move the vertex and the mesh is
ripped. Press Enter to confirm.

Press the A key to deselect all vertices. Suppose you want to patch
up the hole that you created. The solution is to select the vertices
for the new face (3 or 4) and press the F key. To illustrate this,
select the 4 vertices that form the square of the hole created from 2
selected vertices. Press the F key. A face is created.

Press the A key to deselect all vertices. Now we'll create
triangular faces for the remaining two holes. Select the 3 vertices
forming the left triangle, and press F. Press the A key to deselect

everything. Select the 3 vertices forming the right triangle, and press F. The hole is now repaired. Press the A key to deselect.

Ripping via an edge loop is a great way to split a mesh. Select an Edge Loop by positioning the 3D cursor on an edge and pressing ALT+Right Click. Then press the V key and scroll down. Press Enter to confirm. You have now split the mesh along the edge loop.

Rip works in edge mode as well. Go into Edge mode, by either selecting the Edge icon or pressing Control - Tab - 2. Position the 3D cursor above an edge to select. Select the edge (Right Click on an edge). Press the V key. The rip works just like selecting two adjacent vertices, which is, of course, what constitutes an edge.

Press the A key to deselect everything. You rip on two edges along the same loop. Select an unselected edge. Then Shift Select (right click while holding the) to select the edge next to it. Press the V key. The rip works in the trapezoidal fashion you would expect.

Rip works on other meshes as well. Let's look at a UV Sphere. Press tab to go to object mode. Click the second square to go to Level 2, so we have a blank 3D viewport. Add a UV Sphere (Space - Add - Mesh -UVSphere), accepting the default of 32 rings and 32 segments. Press Z to go into wireframe mode. Scale the UVSphere 3 times (S - 3 - Enter). Press Tab to go into Edit mode. Go into Edge select mode (Control - Tab - 2). Press the A key to deselect everything.

Press NUM1 to go to front view. Position the cursor on an edge and press ALT+Right Click to select an edge loop. Position the 3D cursor below the selected loop. Press the V key. Move the selected edge loop down. Behold, you have split the UV Sphere. Press Z to go into solid mode so you can see.

You can also rip and scale at the same time. Select another edge loop (ALT+ Right Click) for splitting the UV Sphere. Position the 3D cursor below the loop. Press the V key, then the Z key to constrain along the Z axis, drag the edge down. Press Enter. Then press the S key to scale the loop.

I hope this gives you a good idea of the Rip tool, which is very handy for creating holes in a mesh. Happy Blendering!

Pixar Eyeball (2.49)

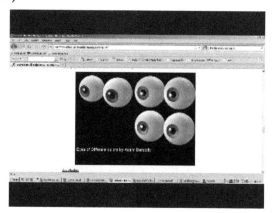

Watch the Video at: http://www.youtube.com/watch?v=52KEN7NJkP0

The goal of this tutorial is to make a Pixar-looking eye. The idea
for this tutorial came from a post by KSF2010 on my Blender 3D Forum,
at http://forum.irakrakow.com. He rendered a whale with "Pixar
eyes". You can see his render at:
http://forum.irakrakow.com/viewtopic.php?f=12&t=235

I was curious how to do Pixar eyes. He mentioned some tutorials on
the web.

This tutorial is based on:
http://en.wikibooks.org/wiki/Blender_3D:_Noob_to_Pro/Creating_Pixar-
looking_eyes_in_Blender

Iris texture: http://en.wikibooks.org/wiki/File:Iris.png

This tutorial uses the same modeling and texturing technique
described in the well-known MAX tutorial by Adam Baroody
(http://www.3dluvr.com/rogueldr/tutorials/eye/eyes.html).

One of the main reasons that Pixar's characters really convey life is
in their eyes. They have depth, you can see how the eye not only
shines but it "collects" light. In this tutorial, we will create a
simple eyeball, without ray tracing, that you can enhance. This is
certainly not the ultimate, final Pixar eyeball render. It's just my
best shot at it. There are 4 parts of the eyeball to render: the
eye white, or sclera, which is the big spherical, oozy shape of the
eye. Then there's the iris, the circular area around the eye. The
pupil is the part of the eye that gives the eye its color. Finally,
the cornea is the semi-transparent enclosure for the iris and the
pupil.

1. Start up Blender. Delete the default cube (Right click to select, press DEL key, Enter to confirm).

2. Add a UV Sphere, with 8 segments and 8 rings.

3. To create the hole at the front of the eyeball, delete the 8 triangular faces that make up one end of the eyeball. Press Tab to go into Edit Mode. Click off the 3D Transform Manipulator. Click on the triangle icon, or press CTRL+Tab-3 to go into face select mode. Press the A key to delect all faces. Press Z to go into Solid Mode. Press the Occlude Background Geometry button because we only want to delete the front faces. Press the B key to go to Border Select mode. Select the middle 8 triangles by creating a rectangle just enclosing the eyeball faces. Press Delete, and select Faces.

4. Let's tweak the eyeball material. Select the eyeball. Press Tab to go to Object mode. Click the Shading Buttons (F5). Select the Material. Make the material color White by setting R=1, G=1, and B=1. In the Shaders tab, dial up the Specularity setting to 1.25 and the Hardness to 165. Click on the Edit button (F9). Click the Set Smooth button. Click the Modifiers tab. Add a Subsurf Modifier at Level 2. These are just my best guess. Experiment until you get the right color, specularity, and hardness.

5. Let's adjust camera and the lighting. In top view, from the View Menu, select Camera, then Align Active Camera to View. Let's move the light closer to the camera. The easiest way to do that is to first, select the camera. Then press SHIFT+S and select Cursor to Selection. Then, select the Lamp. Press SHIFT+S and select Selection to Cursor. This places the light directly at the camera location.

Split the 3D window by right clicking on the bottom border, selecting Split Area, and positioning the cursor, then pressing Enter. Make the right window a camera view. Move the lamp a bit to the side of the camera. Press F12 to render.

6. To make the iris, from the Top View (NUM7), add a circle (Space - Add - Mesh- Circle), with 8 vertices. Tab into Edit Mode. Go to Vertex Select mode by selecting the icon with the dots or pressing CTRL+Tab-1. Press the A key to select all the vertices. Press the E key to extrude, only, don't extrude. Select Edges Only and press Enter. Then press S to scale the extruded circle inside, about 1/4 of the way inward. Press Enter to confirm. Tab into Object Mode.

7. Now add the texture to the iris. Select the Shader button (F5) and click Add New to add a new material. Click the Shadeless button because we are using the image texture without the lights affecting it. We're going to add an image texture for the iris. Press F6 to get to the Texture window. Click Add New. The texture type is Image. Then click Load Image, and select Iris.png, the iris texture on the Blender Noob to Pro tutorial site.

8. To position the iris at the right place, bordering inside the hole of the eyeball, do the following. Select the eyeball. Press SHIFT+S. Select Cursor to Selection. Then select the iris mesh. Press SHIFT+S. Choose Selection -> Cursor. Scale the iris down until you can see it inside the eyeball. Then press the G key, then the Z key, to move the iris up so that it borders the hole. Switch to Camera View (View - Camera, or NUM0). You may have to scale the iris a bit until you get it right.

9. Smooth the iris mesh. Go to the Edit buttons (F9) and press Set Smooth. Then click on Modifiers, and select Subsurf, at Level 1. Press F12 to render.

10. Go to Top View (NUM7). Create a mesh circle, with the default 32 vertices. Extrude the edges (press the E key, the press Enter). Scale the resulting edges inward until they merge close to the center. Add a material, by pressing F5 and clicking the Add New Button. Make the material light blue by making R=0, G=.6, and B=1. Make the material Shadeless so the pupil is not affected by lights. You can, of course, change the color to any one you want.

11. Smooth out the pupil by going to the Edit buttons (F9) and pressing Set Smooth. Click on the Modifiers button, select Subsurf, and give it a Level 1 subsurf.

12. Again, to position the pupil correctly, select the eyeball. Press SHIFT+S. Choose Cursor -> Selection. Select the Pupil. Press SHIFT+S. Choose Selection -> Cursor. Scale the pupil down until you see it from inside the eyeball. Press the G key, then the Z key, and move the pupil until it encloses the rest of the hole. Switch to Camera view to make the final adjustments. Press F12 to render.

13. The cornea is simply a piece that fits exactly in the middle of the hole in the eye white. From the Top View (NUM7), add a circle with 8 vertices (Space - Add - Mesh - Circle). Tab into Edit mode. Make sure all the vertices are selected. If not press the A key until they're all selected. Press the E key, to extrude edges, and press Enter immediately. Then scale the cornea down until the vertices almost touch. Press Tab to go int Object mode.

14. Add a new material by going to the Shading buttons (F5) and clicking Add New. The cornea is a transparent circle that surrounds the iris and the pupil. Let's give it a greenish color, by setting R=.5, G=1, and B=.5. You can set these to anything you want, with the effect of a sort of greenish contact lens color. Set the alpha value of the cornea to .1. In the Shaders tab, set Spec = .6 and Hard = 255. Turn on ZTrans in the Render Pipeline section. Make sure that the 'Traceable' button, under Render Pipeline, in the Links and Pipelines tab, is switched off.

15. Smooth out the cornea by going to the Edit buttons (F9) and pressing Set Smooth. Click on the Modifiers button, selec Subsurf, and give it a Level 1 subsurf.

16. To position the cornea correctly, select the eyeball. Press SHIFT+S. Choose Cursor -> Selection. Select the cornea. Press SHIFT+S. Choose Selection -> Cursor. Scale the cornea down until you see it from inside the eyeball. Press the G key, then the Z key, and move the cornea until it encloses the rest of the hole. Switch to Camera view to make the final adjustments. Press F12 to render.

To create the eye, you need to join the meshes. To do that, change the view on the right to Outline View. Shift Select the eye white, iris, pupil, and cornea. Press CTRL+J to join the meshes. The resulting mesh is your eye. To officially name it, go to the Edit Buttons (F9) and rename the object, in the Ob: section, to Eye. The eye is ready to be placed on your head model, to be animated, or whatever.

A Simple Hat (2.49)

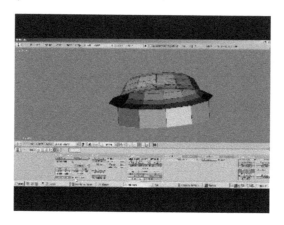

Watch this Video at: http://www.youtube.com/watch?v=-mPtxa_MEPA

This tutorial is based on the Blender 3D Noob to Pro Wikibook Hat
Creation Tutorial, at:
http://en.wikibooks.org/wiki/Blender_3D:_Noob_to_Pro/Creating_a_Simpl
e_Hat. Even though the hat is simple, creating it shows off an
advanced Blender mesh feature, the Spin tool. The wikibook actually
creates the hat as one step in creating a simple person. In this
tutorial, I will just focus on how to create the hat object. We will
create the hat from a mesh circle. Although I used Blender 2.49b,
this tutorial should work in any Blender 2.4x version, because we
will set up the user preferences explicitly.

Steps:

1) Expand the User Preference window by dragging down on its bottom
border. In the Views & Controls panel, enable View Name, so that we
know what view we're working in. Then click on Edit Methods. In the
Add New Objects section, click Aligned to View. This will make
Blender create new objects aligned to whatever view we're in. After
you have made these changes, drag up on the bottom border to contract
the User Preferences to its original position.

2) Delete the default cube. Right click to select, then press X and
Enter to confirm.

3) The 3D View is in Top View, with orthographic projection.
Orthographic projection is best when modeling because the model's
size is not affected by distance. Press Num3 to go to Right Side
view.

4) Press SHIFT+C to place the 3D cursor at 0,0,0. We know the 3D cursor is there because it's at the intersection of the blue line (the Z axis) and the green line (the Y axis).

Press the C key to center the view.

5) Add a circle mesh with 12 vertices, by pressing Space - Add - Mesh - Circle. Change the number of vertices from the default to 12, from the default of 32 vertices. Click OK.

6) Now we are going to make the outline of the hat. It's this outline that we will spin to create the hat. Press Tab to go into Edit Mode. Then, switch to Edge Select mode by either pressing CTRL+Tab and selecting Edges, or clicking on the diagonal line icon that signifies an edge. Delete the three bottom edges by right clicking the first edge, and shift right clicking to add the second and third edges to the section. Then press the X key and select Edges.

7) We're going to move some vertices to create the hat outline. Switch to Vertex Select mode by either pressing CTRL+Tab and selecting Vertices, or clicking on the icon with the little spots that indicate vertex select mode. Disable the transform manipulator by clicking on the hand icon, or by pressing CTRL+Space Bar and selecting Disable.

Right click on the 2 leftmost vertices, one at a time, and press the G key to move them so that they make a hat brim on the left. Then do the same with the 2 rightmost vertices. Move each of them, one at a time, so that they make a hat brim on the right. This is our hat shape, the shape we are going to spin.

8) Before we use the Spin tool, we need to position the 3D cursor in the correct spot. In this case, the 3D cursor needs to be at the rightmost vertex of the hat outline. First select the rightmost vertex. Then press SHIFT+S and choose Cursor -> Selection. The cursor snaps to the rightmost vertex.

9) Now select all the vertices of the outline by pressing the A key twice (the first time, to deselect the rightmost vertex, the second time to select all the vertices of the outline).

10) Press NUM7 to go into Top View. Switch to the Editing panel (F9). In the Mesh Tools tab, find the Spin, Spin Dup and Screw buttons. We need to fill in the fields in the next line to get the Spin tool to create a complete hat. Set Degr to 360 (a full circle rotation), Steps to 12, and Turns to 1 (we only need one turn).

11) Now the magic happens. Click the Spin button. Something happened, but was a hat created. Well, if we press Num3 to go to Right Side view, we see that indeed we did create a hat. What happened was that the outline we created was spun around the Z axis to create the hat. Press F12 to render.

12) We have a hat, but there are is a seam. The reason is that we have duplicate vertices. The Spin actually created two copies of the outline, one at 0 degrees and another at 360 degrees. To fix this problem, press the A key twice to select all the vertices. Then press the W key to bring up the Specials menu. Select Remove Doubles.

13) To make a back visor, go to Edge Select mode, and select the back 4 edges. Press E to extrude the edges, then Z to extrude them in the Z direction, downwards, so it's really the -Z direction. Press F12 to render.

14) To smooth out the hat, to make it look less like a bunch of triangles, from the Edit Menu (F9), in the Links and Materials section, press Set Smooth. Then, in the Modifiers tab, select Subsurf, at Level 3. Then press F12 to render.

There it is...your basic hat shape. You can now add some nice materials and textures, maybe a feather, and shape the hat any way you want.

Importing Google SketchUp .KMZ Files (2.49)

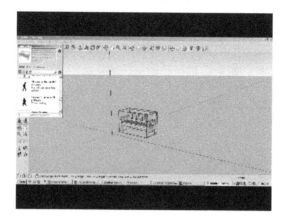

Watch this Video at: http://www.youtube.com/watch?v=ioUzS9b1EkE

The KMZ file is Google's standard file format for models created in
Google Earth, Google 3D Warehouse, and Google SketchUp. The goal of
this tutorial is to show you how to import any of the many thousands
of models from the Google 3D Warehouse, Google Earth, or Google
Sketchup, into Blender. Why reinvent the wheel? It's highly likely
that models such as background scenes, and common objects like chairs
and tables, are already available in these programs. If all you want
is to use these as a background, for your game or animation, why not
import them into Blender?

The secret to doing this is knowing how to import KMZ files. The KMZ
file format is a compressed (actually a zipped) package of files,
which includes the model as a Collada .dae file, as well as the
textures associated with the model. We'll use the World Financial
Center model, in New York City, a detailed model, stored in the
Google 3D Warehouse, at:
http://sketchup.google.com/3dwarehouse/details?mid=a105aae79148f007f1
c45f5a552864cc&ct=hppm. Blender can import KMZ files, preserving the
textures on it, with the Collada plugin. I will show you some tricks
to get the model to render in Blender, as well.

First, let's see the model in Google Earth. This is a simple matter
of telling Google 3D Warehouse to show the model in Google Earth.
Behind the scenes, Google Earth imports the model in kmz format,
uncompressing it and flying to Lower Manhattan, displaying the model.

Next, let's see the model in Google SketchUp. oogle 3D Warehouse
exports the model into SketchUp in SketchUp's native file format,

SKP. If you know how to use Google SketchUp, you can change the model there, and import from Google SketchUp into Blender using the KMZ format. In SketchUp, export the file using File - Import - Google Earth (kmz).

OK. Now let's import the model into Blender 2.49b. These are the steps you need to do:

1) Download the file as kmz.

2) Rename the kmz file to zip.

3) Unzip the zip file. The model is in the Models subdirectory as a dae file.

4) Start up Blender. Run the Collada 1.4 import by selecting Import from the File menu. Then, select Collada .dae 1.4. You need to tell the Collada import where the model is. Navigate to the Model file and select it. Accept the default, which is to Create New Scenes.

Now we're in Blender. It appears that the import was successful. But where is our model? The problem is that SketchUp and Google Earth models are based on actual measurements: feet, inches, meters, centimeters, etc. You really have no control over the dimensions of an imported Collada file. The model may be visible immediately after importing into Blender, or it may not. However, there are techniques that you can work with in Blender to make the model available for your project.

Let's look for our model. First, press the Home key, hoping to find it. No luck. The model isn't there.

Let's split the view, to navigate around using the Outliner. Split the view to make the window on the right an Outline View. Note that the new scene, called SketchUpScene, added the entire model as one mesh, called mesh1. This is a good thing, but it doesn't always happen. Sometimes the model is split into a number of meshes, which makes cleanup a bit more difficult.

The problem is that our view is clipped too short. Select View Properties. Clip End, the end of the clipping area for the viewport, is too small, at 500 Blender units. Set Clip End set at 10000, its maximum value. If that doesn't work, check the Spacing value, defaulted to 1. Bump it up to 20.

Things are starting to get better. If we switch to Front View
(NUM1), we actually see a building which looks like it's part of the
World Financial Center. Let's select the building. It turns out
that the building is a mesh called mesh1. This is not always the
case. Type N to bring up the Transform Properties panel. The model
is at the origin, at its original scale. However, look at the DimX,
DimY, and DimZ values. They're large, because the model is scaled
for Google Earth.

The new scene does have a camera. In the 3D view, press N to bring
up the transform properties panel. Note the camera's position, which
must be somewhere over the Hudson river, I presume.

Here are a few tips, with the camera and the 3D view, that can help
you get the shot you want for the imported model. I'm switching to a
view that I tweaked a bit, that seems to work reasonably well. You
can download the blend file from http://forum.irakrakow.com or from
my blog at http://blender3dvideos.blogspot.com. I rendered it as
well, pressing F12.

1) Add a lamp and parent it to the camera. That way you will have
enough light no matter where you move the camera.

2) Add a Track To constraint on the camera. The best way is to
create an Empty and create the Track To constraint on the empty. See
my video at:

3) Scale the model down so that its dimensions aren't so large.
That should help in terms of appending the model to other scenes.

4) You may want to add a World. In the blend file, since I did not
delete any scenes, you can add the World that comes with the default
scene, or you can create another World from scratch. That can create
a dramatic backdrop for the model.

5) Decreasing the camera lens size will widen the camera's field of
vision, making more of the model visible. Note how the camera's lens
size was decreased from 35, the default, to 10.

6) Display the model in textured mode so you can see how it looks
with textures applied.

7) Try a Camera Fly around. A simple idea is just to press SHIFT+F
and move the camera around. See my Blender Camera Fly Around
tutorial.

Incidentally, the imported model, with its textures, displays fine in the Blender Game Engine. Press P to run the BGE. Press ESC to end the BGE.

Finally, Google SketchUp 7 has many simple components for commonly used objects. Here's a simple example. Start up Google SketchUp 7. Delete the default person, Sang. From the Window menu, choose Components. You can see all sorts of components. Select the bench. You can then export the bench as a 3D model. There's a link in my Forum page for this video where you can see how the bench looks when exported into Blender. The bench is there, textures and all.

I hope this gives you some interesting ideas for importing any of the thousands of well designed and functional models from Google Earth, Google 3D Warehouse, and Google SketchUp, into Blender.

Curve Modeling

Text Objects (2.49)

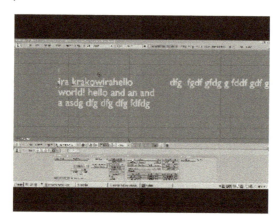

Watch the Video at: http://www.youtube.com/watch?v=IFgHt2mcLK8

Blender's Text object lets you add text to your scene. The text object is actually a type of curve object. Initially, editing text might seem a bit confusing, but, like most things in Blender, it seems logical when you get used to it. At some point, say when you are adding the credits to your movie, you will want to use text objects. The purpose of this tutorial is to help you become comfortable with Blender's text object, showing you how to place text precisely. I used Blender 2.49b for this tutorial.

To add text, you press Space - Add - Text. You are in object mode. Like other Blender objects, you can rotate, scale, and grab the text object. To illustrate this, press the G key to grab the object, and move it. Press the R key to rotate the text. Then, press the S key to scale the text. This can produce dramatic effects like floating text in 3D space. You can clear the rotation by pressing ALT+R and set the location to (0,0,0) by pressing ALT+G.

To change the text, press Tab to go into Edit mode. The text changes to a grey color. To move the cursor, you use the arrow keys on the typewriter keypad, NOT the arrow keys on the numeric keypad. Pressing left arrow moves the cursor back one character. Pressing right arrow moves the cursor forward one character. The Home key gets you to the beginning of the text and the End key gets you to the end of the text.

You can change the text, which by default is the word "Text". The backspace key erases a character and moves the cursor backwards one character. I'll delete the word Text, one character at a time, and type in my name, Ira Krakow. You can add special characters, which are accessed from the Char tab. ALT+G, for example, adds the degree symbol. If your keyboard supports another language, you can also add characters in that language by pressing the Unicode button and selecting your language. Blender fully supports international characters.

The text object has an internal clipboard which works slightly different from the Windows clipboard. I'll copy my first name to the text buffer. First, press the Home key to get to the beginning of the text. Then hold down the shift key and press the right arrow key on the typewriter. The I is highlighted in black, indicating that it is part of the selection. Continue to hold the and press right arrow again. Now the "r" is highlighted as well. Press the and the right arrow key again. Now my name, Ira, is highlighted. To copy my name, press CTRL+C. Press the End key to move the cursor to the end of the text. To paste my name, press CTRL+V.

You can apply special effects to part of the text selection. Select Krakow by holding the and pressing the arrow keys until my name is selected. To underline just that part of the text, press the U button or press CTRL+U.

CTRL+Left Arrow moves the cursor back to the beginning of the previous word. CTRL+Right arrow moves the cursor forward to the beginning of the next word.

What's not immediately apparent is that Blender places text in frames. Initially, when I saw the Left, Center, Right, and Justify buttons, I was confused because I did not see any reference to a line length. Think of a frame as like a container. Initially, the frame is not visible because its width and height are 0 and the text does not word wrap. This can get messy if you enter a lot of text. Blender allows up to 50,000 characters in a text object but you'll be hard pressed to see all of them as you scroll right.

You can insert text from a file. To illustrate that, I created a file with the text Hello World in it. I position the cursor at the end of the text and click on Insert File. I navigate to the file, press Enter, and the text is inserted.

To set a frame, use the width and the height settings. The settings are in Blender Units, not characters. To see the frame, set the width and/or height to a number greater than 0. Go to the Width setting and set it to 10. You now see a horizontal line of 10 Blender Units display. Now the buttons that confused me make sense. Press the Left button. The text is left aligned. Press the Right button. The text is right aligned. Press the Center button. The text is centered. Press the Flush button. The text is spread out across the width of the line. The ToUpper button converts the text to upper case. Pressing the ToUpper button again converts the text back to its original case.

Let's see how height works. Go to the Height setting and set it to 3. Press the Left button to left align the text. Now start typing. When the text overflows the line, it goes to the next line. However, as you type more text, eventually the text overflows the box.

We can control where the overflow text goes by inserting another frame. Note that the second frame overlaps the first frame. However, by adjusting the X and Y offset you can control where the second part of the text displays. Set the x to 1 and the Y to -3 and you can see that the text is positioned below the previous text, each text area controlled by its frame. Two column text is easy. Set x to 11, to move it over to the beginning of the second column, and y to 0. You can adjust the width and the height of the second frame as well, giving you precise control over the column layout.

The default font is a built in 11 point font. You can change the font to another font that is on your computer by going to the Font panel and clicking on the Load button. Navigate to the directory containing the fonts. On my Windows Vista computer, the fonts are located in the C:\Windows\Fonts directory. After you navigate to the directory, the available fonts are prefixed with a blue dot. You can select the font and click on the SELECT FONT button.

If the font supports it, you turn on italics by pressing CTRL+I or pressing the I button next to the font. You turn on bold by pressing CTRL+B or pressing the B button next to the font. You turn on underscore by pressing CTRL+U or pressing the U button next to the font.

A text object has no depth. To give it depth, in the Curve and Surfaces panel, give it an Extrude value greater than 0. You can also bevel the edges by setting the Bevel size to a number greater than 0. Tab out of object mode and you can see the depth and the bevel.

You can convert a font to a curve or a mesh. To do this, press ALT+C and select either the curve or the Mesh option. If you choose Mesh, then the text now can be manipuluated as if it were a mesh.

You can have different parts of the text have different colors. To illustrate this, load the default scene by going to the File Menu and selecting Load Factory settings. Delete the default cube. Add a text object (Space - Add - Text). Press tab to go into edit mode. Delete the default text and add the text Ira Was Here. Let's make Ira red, Was green, and Here blue. To do this, go to the Edit buttons (F9), and add 3 material slots by pressing the New button in the Links and Materials panel 3 times. Click the left arrow 2 times to get to the first material. Press the Shading buttons (F5) and click Add New to add a material, and make it Red. Go back to the Edit buttons (F9) and click Assign. The entire text turns red.

Now highlight the word Was. Select the second material. Press the Shading buttons (F5), then Add New, to add a new material, and make it green. Go back to the Edit buttons (F9) and click Assign. Now the word Was is green.

Highlight the word Here by pressing the right arrow key and highlighting each letter, holding the shift key to add to the selection as you press the right arrow key. Select a third material slot. Go to the Shading buttons, press Add New, and make this material blue. Now Ira is red, Was is green, and Here is blue.

A neat feature of a text object is that it can be wrapped to follow a curve. Tab out of edit mode. Locate the 3D cursor in another part of the scene. Add a Bezier Circle (Space - Add - Curve - Bezier Circle). Scale the circle up to 3 times its size (S 3 Enter).

The circle is called CurveCircle. Select the Text object. In the Curve and Surfaces panel, find the TextOnCurve area. In that area, enter CurveCircle, the name of the Bezier circle. The text is now rounded according to the shape of the circle. If you select the circle and scale it, the text scales accordingly.

I hope this tutorial has increased your comfort level with text objects. Happy Blending!

Halloween Mask Using Bezier Curves (2.49)

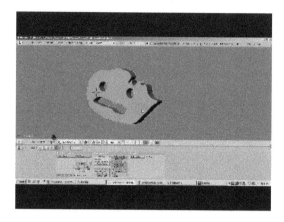

Watch the Video at: http://www.youtube.com/watch?v=Vf-s7TySVu8

Modeling with curves is a powerful Blender features. Few objects in life are pure straight lines. Life continues to throw curves at us. As an example, we're going to make a Halloween mask with Bezier curves.

Blender itself uses Bezier curves extensively. The curves in the IPO window, as an example, are Bezier curves. So if you're going to be animating your scene, you can do a lot more if you understand how to manipulate Bezier curves. There are also some great modeling tools, such as loft modeling and beveling, which rely on Bezier curves. Knowing how to deal with Bezier curves is a fundamental Blender skill.

Start with the default Blender scene and delete the default cube by right clicking it, pressing the DEL key, and confirming the delete. We'll work first with a special case of the Bezier curve, the Bezier circle. A Bezier circle is a Bezier curve that just happens to be a circle as well. Like all Bezier curves, and also like mesh objects, the Bezier circle can be moved, scaled, and rotated.

How does the Bezier circle differ from the mesh circle? A mesh circle is defined with a certain number of vertices. The more vertices, the closer the circle looks like a circle. Of course, it's never a perfect circle. You pay a price for more geometry in terms of rendering time and modeling complexity.

A Bezier circle is a true circle, as opposed to a circle mesh, which never can be an exact circle because it's composed of straight edges. We can increase the number of vertices, do smoothing, and other tricks to make it render close to a circle, but it's never an exact circle. Also, mesh circles have modeling problems such as dark edges where normals are inside the mesh, instead of outside the mesh, where the edge can render with light.

Delete the Bezier circle. We'll look at the more general case of Bezier curves. Our goal is to create a mask using Bezier curves, and then to convert it to a mesh.

Start with adding the Bezier curve, with SPACE - Add - Curve - Bezier Curve. A Bezier curve is a curved line called a spline. At either end are control vertices, which you can select, grab, and move around. In addition to the control vertices, one at either end, there are lines that extend out, which are called control handles. You can select a handle, move it in or out. You control the shape of the curve by controlling the handle. The handle on the left controls the shape of the spline coming in. The handle on the right controls the shape of the spline coming out.

You can add vertices by pressing the Control key while left clicking with your mouse. We'll add a few vertices to start the face. The handles on either side of the control vertices are purple lines. The handles by default are align handles. The other handle aligns with the one you select. You can change from Align to Free by pressing the H key. The handles turn black and you can turn each one individually. One handle controls how the curve moves into the control vertex, the other controls how the curve move out of the control vertex.

For creating a simple outline, the easiest choice is Auto, which you turn on with SHIFT+H. Auto automatically smooths out the curve coming in and out of the spline. So we'll turn on Auto with Shift H.

CTRL+LMB creates an additional control vertex, so you can make a shape from an outline. We'll make the face part of the mask first. Then we'll cut out the eyes and the mouth. We'll add more splines to the curve. You can use the handles to control the shape of the curve. You can select a vertex, in which case the handles are selected as well. You can control the curve path through the handles as well.

When you're done with the outline, and you want to close the curve, select a vertex and press the C key. The curve then closes.

You can create straight line handles easily. Select two adjacent vertices and press the V key. V is for Vector. This makes the curve become a straight line. Press CTRL+Z to undo this because our mask doesn't have straight lines. Frequently, you will have to model an object, such as a wineglass, that is a mixture of straight lines and curves.

You can still edit the face and add more depth to it.

By default, you control the curve in 2D space. You can't move it in 3D space unless you go to the Curve and Surfaces panel and switch on the 3D button. Then you can grab one of the control vertices and move it in 3D space.

We can also make the mask 3D. Turn on the 3D button and you will see perpendicular lines, like a porcupine, jutting out of the curve. You can extend the curve into 3D if you want.

Now we'll add two eyes, which will be Bezier circles. Do Space-Add-Curve-Bezier Circle. Scale down the circle and press the G key to move it to where the left eye should be. Note that there's a hole cut out of the face for the eye. Press SHIFT+D to duplicate the circle. Press the G key and position the second circle to where the right eye should be.

Let's make the mouth using another Bezier curve. Do Space, Add-Curve-Bezier Curve. Press SHIFT+H to go into Auto mode. Add vertices - CTRL+LMB - until the shape of the mouth looks right. Then press C to close the curve. Select the vertices of the inner circle, press the S key to scale the mouth. Go into object mode.

The Bezier patch is 2D. Let's extrude the mask to give it some depth. As you increase the Extrude value, the mask gets thicker. You can also bevel the mask to round out the edges. The mask can still be edited as you go.

It's time to turn our mask into a mesh object. To do this, tab out of edit mode, and to convert it, do ALT+C to convert to a mesh. From there, all the mesh functions are available. We'll smooth it and add a subsurf modifier. We can do a lot more, in fact, such as changing to face mode and extruding some faces to create a nose, or grabbing some faces and moving them.

To sum up, working with curves is a powerful addition to your modeling arsenal. If you can visualize your object from a curved outline, using curves, including Bezier curves, is a powerful way to create a Blender object from your outline.

Camera and Lighting

Camera Controls (2.5)

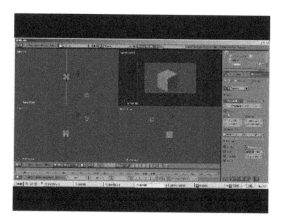

Watch the Video at: http://www.youtube.com/watch?v=O3_SC3xH96o

The purpose of this video is to demonstrate the camera controls in Blender 2.5. The controls are similar to Blender 2.4x. 2.5, at least my pre-alpha release as of mid-September, adds some interesting controls, notably the Panorama lens, simulating a 360 degree fisheye lens. You could follow along with a 2.4x Blender version, although you would need to either create your own version of Quad View or just follow me with your own 3D view.

The camera settings are grouped in the Object Data icon for the camera object. In 2.4x, highlight the camera (right click), and press F9 for the Edit buttons. Since the controls are very similar, if you know your way around the Blender 2.4x camera, you should be able to become comfortable with Blender 2.5's camera very quickly. I don't think you can buy a camera with all of Blender's features. You can get some interesting effects by adjusting its controls, which might be easier than moving the camera.

We'll start with the 2.5 default scene, and highlight the camera. This demo works best in the new Quad View. From the View Menu, select Toggle Quad View to see the scene from Top, Front, Right, and Camera views simultaneously.

Look at the Camera View, in the upper right corner of the 3D viewport. The camera is in Perspective mode and the cube is in the center. Press F12 to render.

The camera controls are located in the Object Data area of the Properties Window (formerly known as the Buttons Window). By default, Blender renders the camera in perspective view, where parallel lines meet at a vanishing point. The lens angle defaults to 35 millimeters, a standard camera lens. Increasing the angle causes the camera to zoom into the cube. Decreasing the angle causes the camera to zoom out. You can choose degrees instead of millimeters, if you wish. Here's the scene rendered from a 100 degree camera lens.

Press the Orthographic button. The camera now is in Orthographic view, where parallel lines do not meet. Below the Perspective / Orthographic buttons is the Orthographic Scale area, set to 7.314. If you lower the scale setting, it's as if the camera zooms into the cube. If you raise the scale setting, it's as if the camera zooms out and the cube is farther away from the camera. This is a way of changing the camera's view without actually moving the camera.

Check the Panorama check box and press F12 to render. The result is a cube as if it was shot with a 360 degree panoramic fisheye type lens.

Turn off the Panorama check box and switch back to Perspective view.

Go to the Display area and check the Limits button. Limits gives each view a line showing how far, in Blender units, the camera sees. You can control what the camera sees by changing the Clipping Start and Clipping End parameters. Clipping Start, defaulting to .1, is the number of Blender units where the camera starts to see. Clipping End, defaulting to 100, is the number of Blender units up to where the camera sees. Change Clipping End to 5 and press F12 to render. The cube does not render because the camera's view is clipped before it sees the cube. You can see that the camera's clipping end is before it sees the cube. Increase Clipping End until the camera can see part of the cube, at 10 Blender units or so. Then press F12 to render. Incidentally, the camera view shows how much, if any, of the cube, will render. Now the a part of the cube is rendered. Press Z to go to wireframe mode, so we can see the inside of the cube. Increase the camera's Clipping End to 11 and press F12 to render. We see even more of the cube. Finally, with clipping end at 12, the camera can see the entire cube.

The Passepartout check box, which is on by default, is a visual way of showing what part of the scene the camera sees. In 2.4x, Passsepartout is off by default. Uncheck the Passepartout check box. The entire camera area is shaded uniformly, so you would not know what the camera see unless you render the scene.

Check the Passepartout check box. The alpha slider underneath Passepartout controls the transparency (alpha of 0, means fully transparent, alpha of 1 means fully opaque) of the passepartout area - how much of the scene under it is shown.

Check the Title Safe button, which is off in 2.5 but on in 2.4x. Title Safe is a dashed line which shows the limits of the area that would display on certain television screens. Don't worry about it unless you are planning to distribute your video to television. Even here, Title Safe only applies to certain types of televisions. Uncheck the Title Safe button to show what will render. Move the cube to the upper left corner of the Passepartout area and press F12 to render. The cube actually renders in that area.

Highlight the camera and go back to the camera controls settings.

The Shift X and Shift Y settings allow you to adjust the camera viewing area without moving the camera, similar to you adjusting a real camera.

Check the Name button. This shows the camera name - Camera - in the 3D viewport.

Size is size of the icon, defaulting to .5 Blender units used for the camera icon. It has no effect on the rendering. You may want a bigger or smaller camera icon in your scene. Note the filled in triangle at the top of the camera. The fact that the triangle is filled in means that this camera is the active camera, the one that will be used when the scene is rendered.

Although you can have as many cameras as you like, only one active camera is allowed in Blender. To illustrate, select the camera and press SHIFT+D to duplicate. Then move the new camera to another part of the scene. The new camera has a hollow triangle instead of a filled in triangle, which means that it is not the active camera. In Blender 2.4x, you could make the new camera the active camera by pressing CTRL+ALT+NUM0. My pre-alpha version of Blender does not have this functionality yet. You need at least one camera to render a scene. In Blender 2.4x you would get the "Error-No Camera" message if you did not have a camera and pressed F12. In Blender 2.5, no error message is produced, but you don't get a render either.

The Mist check box shows the mist area for the camera, if Mist is on. To illustrate, I'll move the cube back towards the center of the scene. Then, we go to the World buttons, turn on the Mist check box there to enable mist. Set the start of the effect at 1 and the end at 11. Press F12 to render. Part of the cube is shown, the other part is shrouded in mist.

Depth of field can be set for an object, or in Blender units. It determines where the focus of the camera is. Depth of Field can be set in Blender units, or you can specify an object on which the camera will focus. We'll set Depth of Field to the Cube object. DOF won't affect the render unless we use nodes, with the Defocus Filter or a blurring type of filter. We'll save that discussion for another time.

The Blender 2.5 camera can produce interesting effects to make your scenes more realistic.

Camera Changer Script (2.49)

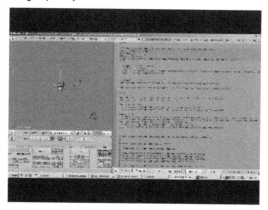

Watch the Video at: http://www.youtube.com/watch?v=6UdG7ClEU5A

Adding cameras, which have different views of the scene, and then changing them during your animation, can add more drama and realism to your animations. Blender lets you have as many cameras as you want, and to position them anywhere in your scene. Blender also has many Python scripts. You've probably used a few of them. For example, if you have ever saved the UV face layout from the UV/Image editor, to export the UV face layout to an image editor, you've used a Python script.

As it happens, there's a Python script, called camera_changer.py, that lets you change the active camera at any frame that you want. The script is easy to use, relying on a simple naming convention for each camera. In good old Blender tradition, we'll animate Suzanne and, at different frames in the animation, change the animation so that we look at her from the default camera, then from above, and finally from below. After that, we'll go behind the scenes so to speak and we'll look at the Python script that does all the magic.

So start with the default Blender scene. Delete the default cube by right clicking on the cube, pressing Delete, and then pressing Enter. Add Suzanne, the Blender mascot (Space - Add - Mesh - Monkey). Press F10 to bring up the Scene buttons. Click the Preview button at the extreme right, so that we get a 640 x 480 render size, making the rendering time fairly quick. Click the Render button to render. We're at Frame 1 and we get a view of Suzanne from about a 45 degree angle.

Now we'll add two cameras, one looking down at Suzanne, the other looking up at her. To do that, go to Front view, which makes the blue direction up and down. Position the 3D cursor at 0,0,0 by pressing SHIFT+C. Add a camera (Space - Add - Camera). Move the camera upward in the blue direction 5 Blender units (G Z 5 Enter). From the View menu, select Cameras, and then Select Active Object as Active Camera. Press F12 to render. Now you have a head on shot of Suzanne.

Add a third camera by selecting the camera and pressing SHIFT+D. Move this camera 10 units down in the Z direction (G Z -10 Enter). Rotate the camera 180 degrees so it's looking upwards (R 180 Enter). From the View menu, select Cameras, and then Select Active Object as Active Camera. Press F12 to render. Now we see the back of Suzanne's head.

Now the fun begins. From the Front view (NUM1), go to the Animation set up by selecting it from the default Blender 2.49 setups. Note that there are 3 cameras, Camera (the original one), Camera.001 (the camera looking from the top), and Camera.002 (the camera looking from the bottom). We're going to make the default Camera active at Frames 1, 101, and 201. Camera.001 will be active at Frames 50, 125, and 225. Camera.002 will be active at Frames 75, 175, and 240. Camera_changer.py looks at the camera names to determine when to change the active camera. The frame numbers are separated by commas. Rename Camera to 1,101,201 from the Outliner (CTRL+LMB, then rename). Left click on Camera.001. Rename it to 50,125,225 by control left clicking and entering those numbers. Then left click on Camera.002. Rename it to 75,175,240.

To activate the camera_changer script, go to the Scripts setup by selecting it. Click the Scripts button. Under Animation, choose Camera Changer. Note in the lower right window, the Enable Script Links button is now enabled. In addition, the Camera_changer.py script has been selected, for the Frame Changed event. What this means is that this script runs every time a the next frame is rendered. Camera_changer simply checks the list of frames in the camera name to figure out if the active camera needs to be changed. There are other events - OnLoad, OnSave, Render, and Redraw - from which a Python script can run.

That's it. To render the animation, press CTRL+F12. Watch the cameras change.

Let's look under the hood. Change the Script window to the Text window. From the Text menu, select Open. Navigate to the Blender Scripts directory. Sometimes that directory is hidden. On my Vista machine, it's in the AppData, Roaming folder, which is hidden. You need to make sure you can see the directory.

Here's the code. At the top, in the area I highlight in pink, are some comments conforming to the Blender convention, with the headings Name, Heading, Blender, and Tip. The name (Camera Changer) is the script's name. Blender is the Blender version it was coded for. Group (Animation) is the Script group from where you can select the script. Tip is help text for the script.

The real action in the script takes place in the main() function, which I highlight in pink. Basically, the Blender module contains all the functions you can call with Python. The code gets the current scene, gets the frame number, and checks the list of objects in the scene. If the object is a camera, and if the current frame number is in the list of frame numbers of the camera name, the SetCurrentCamera() function is called to make that camera the active camera.

In case you're wondering, this other main() function installs the scriptlink for camera_changer.py. It was called, once, when you chose camera_changer.py. This sets up camera_changer to run.

As an aside, I absolutely guarantee you that this script will NOT run in Blender 2.5. First of all, this script runs in Python 2.6, while Blender 2.5 runs Python 3. A simple thing like the print statement needs to be enclosed in parentheses. Second, and actually more important, the Blender module is not currently supported in Blender 2.5. The API has been completely rewritten and is encapsulated in the bpy module. It's entirely possible that this camera changer script will NEVER run in Blender 2.5.

So it's pretty simple to change cameras. I hope you are inspired to become the next Alfred Hitchcock by this.

Positioning the Camera (2.49)

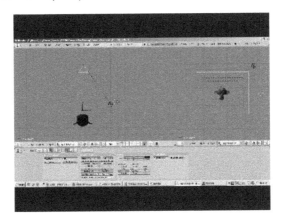

Watch the Video at: http://www.youtube.com/watch?v=NzEy2sCZcHo

Positioning the camera is a vital part of rendering a scene. In this tutorial, I will show you how to position the camera so that you can focus it on a particular object, as well as to move it around so that you can render the scene from close up, from far away, or at any angle. I will also show how to do a "fly around" - animating the camera as if it was flying above the ground, alternating from close up to far away. I used Version 2.49b in this tutorial.

First, we will create the objects in the scene. Delete the default cube (right click, X key, then Enter to confirm). Add a monkey (SPACE - Add - Mesh - Monkey). Make the monkey green by pressing the Shading buttons (F5), then material subcontext, and click Add New. Set the RGB colors to R=0, G=1 and B=0. Press Tab to go to Edit Mode. Go to the Edit buttons (F9). Press the Set Smooth button to smooth the monkey mesh out. Press F9 to go into object mode.

We will now set up the camera with adequate light. Press the Home key to show all the objects in the scene. Let's see how the lamp works. Use the Shaded Mode draw type so we can see how the lamp shades the monkey. Move the lamp around the monkey to see how the lamp causes different parts of the monkey to be highlighted.

Press NUM1 to go to Front View. Move the lamp close to the camera. Make the lamp the child of the camera, so that the lamp will follow the camera. This will insure that no matter where the camera goes, there is enough light. This setup is similar to old fashioned cameras, where a little light is attached to the camera. To make the lamp the child of the camera, select the lamp first (right click).

Then press SHIFT+Right Click and select the camera. Press CTRL+P to make the camera the parent of the lamp. Note the dash line between the camera and the lamp, indicating the parent-child relationship.

Camera and light set up can get complicated. We're going to look at some simple setups that hopefully will get you started. To start, split the 3D viewport horizontally, making the right view a camera view. One simple idea is to have the camera follow the monkey around. To do this, select the camera, and go to the Object button (F7). Go to the Constraints panel (at the extreme right), and click the Add Contraint button. Choose the Track To constraint. Go to the OB: button and type the name of the Monkey, Suzanne.

We need to tell the camera how to align itself with respect to Suzanne. Press the last Minus sign, which means the -Z direction. In Blenderspeak, -Z means down. In the Up: section, click on Y (X would work as well). Now, no matter where we move the camera, Suzanne is in view. We can do a close up or go far away, or move to an angle.

More often, you're not focusing on one object, but instead you want to move the camera around the scene without moving any object in particular. To do this, create an empty object and track the camera to it. We'll create an empty object, which is just a point in space, at 0,0,0. Press SHIFT+C to position the cursor at 0,0,0. Then press Space - Add - Empty to add the empty object, which is named, appropriately enough, Empty. Select the camera. Go back to the Track To constraint, delete the word Suzanne, and add the word Empty. Now the camera follows the empty object instead of Suzanne. To illustrate this, select the Empty object, move it around, and watch what happens in camera view. We can also select the camera and move it around for a close up or a far away shot, or anything in between. This setup is much more flexible than locking the camera on Suzanne.

Finally, we'll look at animating the camera so that it flies around the monkey. Delete the camera's Track To constraint.

First, select the camera. Before we place it on the path, we need to set its rotation and location to zeroes. Press ALT+G to set its location to 0,0,0. Press ALT+R to set its rotation to 0. Press the Z key to go into wireframe mode.

Now we're ready to create the path around which the camera will follow. To do this, press SHIFT+C to position the cursor at 0,0,0. Add a Bezier circle (Space - Add - Curve - Bezier Circle). Scale it up 4 times (S 4 Enter) so that it forms a big circle around Suzanne. Go to the Edit buttons (F9). Press the CurvePath button. This makes the Bezier circle act as a path for the camera. The Pathlen determines how many frames the animation will take. Keep it at 100.

Also, turn off the Back and Front buttons so that the circle doesn't render. The object, by the way, is named CurveCircle.

Now select the camera. Go to the Object buttons (F7). Press CTRL+Down Arrow to make the buttons window full screen. Add a constraint to the camera. Select the Follow Path constraint, and set the object to CurveCircle. Click the third minus sign for -Z, and the Y button in the Up: area.

Now add another constraint, the Track To constraint on the Empty, that we had before. Click the Add Constraint button. Select the Track To constraint. As with the Follow Path constraint, click the third minus sign, for -Z, and the Y button in the Up area. Press SHIFT+ALT+A. The camera should follow the path of the Bezier circle, but it's not yet pointing at Suzanne because it is below her.

To fix this, move the Bezier circle path above the monkey by selecting the circle, pressing the G key, and then then the Z key to constrain on the Z axis.

Press SHIFT+ALT+A to animate. The camera circles around the monkey, following the path.

The animation stops at Frame 100 and pauses until Frame 250. To fix this, go to the Scene buttons (F10) and set the End frame to 100. In the camera view, press SHIFT+ALT+A.

To summarize, we now can focus the camera on a specific object, focus the camera on an empty object, and move the empty (or the camera) to get various views of the scene, and we have animated the camera around a path, similar to flying around over a scene. I hope this gives you some ideas for camera positioning in Blender. Happy Blending!

Depth of Field With Nodes (2.49)

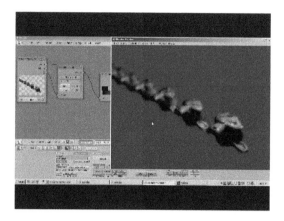

Watch the Video at: http://www.youtube.com/watch?v=HBomEv-bEtw

The eye naturally focuses on sharper objects in a scene and tends to overlook blurred objects. Depth of Field (DOF) is a technique in which you highlight objects in focus, giving them the illusion of being closer to the camera, and blur out the parts of the scene that are not as important. You can use this to force your viewers to focus on the objects you consider important. Using Blender's composite nodes, with some mathematical trickery, you can set up Depth of Field.

So let's get started. Fire up Blender, delete the default cube (Right Click, DEL key, and Enter to confirm). Add the monkey mesh (Space - Add - Mesh - Monkey). Let's make the monkey green. Press F5 (Shading). Then click Add New to add a new material. Set R=0, G=1, and B=0. Go to the Edit buttons (F9). Press the Set Smooth button to make Suzanne more presentable.

Let's make more Suzannes. Click the Modifier button, at the extreme right. Add an Array Modifier. Make sure Relative Offset is clicked. Set X= -1, Y=0, and Z=0. Set Count = 8. Press F12 to render. We now have 8 monkeys, each a bit farther away from the camera than the previous one. The last two monkeys are out of camera range. To fix this, press N to bring up the Transform Properties window. Set LocX to 3. Now there are 8 monkeys in camera range.

Suppose we want our viewers to focus on the first monkey and gradually blur the rest of them as they get further from the camera. We can achieve this effect with Composite Nodes. To do this, change the window type of the 3D Viewport to Node Editor. We start out with

two nodes. The input Render Layers node is our original scene before
the composite node magic is applied. The output Composite node is
the final, composited result. Move the Composite node all the way to
the right.

Add a Map Value node (Space - Add - Vector - Map Value). Map Value
takes information and maps it into a range of values. Map Value can
also add a number (the Offset), as well as multiply by a number (the
Scale) from the input. We're going to play with the offset and scale
in a minute. In this case, we are going to map the Z value, which is
the distance, in Blender Units, of each pixel, from the camera.
Connect the Z socket of the Render Layers node to the Value socket of
the Map Value node.

Next, add a Color Ramp node (Space - Add - Converter - ColorRamp).
The color ramp gives us a visual representation of the Z values, with
values from 0 (black) to 1 (white), Connect the Map Value's Value
socket to the Factor socket of the Color Ramp node. Then, connect
the ColorRamp image socket to the Composite Node image socket.

Right now the compositor shows all white. That's because all the
monkeys map to a value of 1 or greater. The first monkey is about 5
Blender Units from the camera. With this mapping, the monkeys all
map to white.

However, if we adjust the offset to -6 and the Size to .1, we get an
interesting falloff from black to white. What happens is that for
distances between 6 and 16 Blender units, we map a value between 0
and 1. Here's an example. Take a pixel at 10 Blender Units from the
camera. First subtract 6, to get 4, then multiply 4 by .1, yielding
a value of .4, which maps to a grayish color 40% between black and
white. Any Z distance less than 6 produces black. A value greater
than 16 produces white. We can translate this falloff into a gradual
blurring.

To do this, add a Blur node (Space - Add - Filter - Blur). Connect
the Image socket of the Render Layer node to the Image socket of the
Blur node. That will feed the original scene to the blur node.
Then, connect the Image socket of the ColorRamp node to the Size
socket of the Blur node, feeding the adjusted Z values to the Blur
node. Connect the Image socket of the Blur node to the Image socket
of the Composite node.

You need to fiddle around with the X and Y values in the blur node to
set up the exact amount of blur falloff. I found that X=6 and Y=6
worked well for focusing on the first monkey and gradually fading out
the others.

We're ready to render. Go to the scene buttons (F10). Press the Do Composite button to tell the Renderer that we are using composite nodes. Press F12 to render. You should get the depth of field effect we're aiming for.

That's it. I hope this gives you some interesting ideas for highlighting objects in your scene using depth of field. Happy Blendering!

Ray Mirror (2.49)

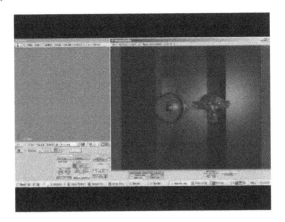

Watch this Video at: http://www.youtube.com/watch?v=aoOmD5k4QkU

Ray tracing casts simulated rays of light on the scene and is on by default in Blender 2.49. Ray tracing gives the most realistic light properties in Blender, but the renders take the longest. That is why all of my renders in this video will be time lapsed. Don't expect the same rendering times as you see in this video, unless you work for Pixar or the Defense Department. For many animation and game engine applications, ray tracing rendering times are unacceptably slow. In other videos, we will discover alternatives, such as Z buffering, for which response times are more acceptable. However, the effects won't be as realistic as with ray mirror. In this video, we will be looking at a special type of ray tracing effect, ray mirror, which creates mirror reflections.

When a ray of light hits the surface of an object, one of three things can happen. The light can be absorbed by the object, the light can pass through the object (if the object has some transparency), or the light can be reflected back, which is what happens with a mirror. In reality, most objects have a combination of absorption, transparency, and reflective properties. Think of a blue light bulb. The light bulb looks blue because some of the light is absorbed by the material, glass or otherwise, to make it look blue. Perhaps you can see part of the inside of the light bulb, say if it is not frosted, such as the filament. That's because the light bulb has some transparent properties. Finally, if you can see part of the background through the light bulb, that's because of its mirror like, reflective properties. Ray Mirror controls this last property.

To show how Ray Mirror works, start up Blender and delete the default cube. Select the cube, press the DEL key and press Enter to confirm. Make sure you are in Top View by pressing NUM7. Add a plane (Space - Add - Mesh - Plane). Scale the plane 5 times (S - 5 - Enter). The plane is going to act as a mirror. To make this happen, with the full Ray Mirror effect, press the Shading buttons (F5) and use the default material (Material). Click the Mirror Trans tab, then click the Ray Mirror button, and turn RayMir to 1. RayMir is a slider which goes from 0 to 1, representing 0% to 100% as a decimal number. Give the plane a red color (R=1, G=0, B=0).

Position the camera directly at the plane with View - Align View - Align Active Camera to View.

Go to Front View (NUM1). Press the Home key to see all the objects, particularly, the camera. Duplicate the plane (SHIFT+D). Move the plane upwards, in the Z direction (press the G key and then the Z key), so that it is behind the camera. The duplicated plane has Ray Mirror on as well.

Go to the Scene buttons (F10). Make sure the Ray button is turned on, so that Ray Tracing is enabled.

Center the 3D cursor by pressing SHIFT+C. Add the monkey (Space - Add - Mesh - Monkey). Add a new material by pressing F5 (Shaders) and clicking the Add New button. Make Suzanne green (R=0, G=1, B=0). Move the monkey 1 Blender unit to the right and up a bit. Go to Edit buttons (F9). Press the Set Smooth button. Add a Subsurf Level 2, Render Level 3.

Make sure you are in Object Mode. If not, press the tab key. Add a UV Sphere (Space - Add - Mesh - UVSphere). Give the UV Sphere a blue color by going to the Shaders panel (F5), adding a new material (Add New button) and setting R=0, G=0, and B=1. Move the UV Sphere 2 Blender units to the left and up a bit, off the floor of the plane. Press F9 to go to the Edit buttons. Click the Set Smooth button to smooth out the UV Sphere.

Press F12 to render. The red mirror should show the mirroring of both the monkey and the UV Sphere, as the light bounces off the bottom mirror, sees the monkey and the UV Sphere, and then the objects are mirrored off the top mirror. The shadow obscures somewhat the mirrored effect.

Let's turn off shadows. Go to the Scene buttons (F10) and click off
Shadow. Press F12 to render. Now you get the effect of both the top
mirror and the bottom mirror.

The mirror effect can be combined with the color effect. Select
either mirror plane (Right click). Press F5 to access the Shaders
buttons. In the Ray Mirror group, turn Ray Mirror to 0. Press F12
to render. There is no mirror effect. The monkey and the UV Sphere
both render, and the plane is red.

Now set Ray Mirror to .5, so we get half mirror and half color.
Press F12 to render. Now the red base color shows through, but the
mirror effect shows through as well. You can play with Ray Mirror to
get the combination you like.

The mirror color can also play a role. Turn Ray Mirror back to 1 so
we get the full ray mirror effect. Now let's set the mirror color to
yellow. Select the Mirror color rectangle, and change it to Yellow
(R=1, G=1, B=0). Press F12 to render. We get a really interestng
result. The yellow mirror color mixes with the material's color.
The monkey is green. Yellow already has green. So the mirrored
monkey remains green. However, the sphere is blue. The mirror
color, yellow, has no blue, so the mirrored UV sphere is yellow. By
the way, there's also a blending with the sky color, which is also
mirrored, which accounts for the color variation outside the mirror
boundary.

The Depth setting controls how many times the mirror effect bouncing
is produced. Let's crank up the depth to 5 and press F12 to render.
There are now more mirrored monkeys and UV Spheres.

The Fresnel setting produces another interesting effect, mixing the
mirror color, and the mirror's diffuse color. Let's crank Fresnel to
1.5 and render.

The Glossiness setting affects the blurriness of the reflection. The
default of 100% glossiness produces a crisp reflection. A little bit
of reduction goes a long way in increasing the realism of the render.
Set glossiness to .9 (90%) and you'll get an effect that simulates a
bit of dirt in the mirror.

There's more. How about turning on Ray Mirror for the monkey and the
UV Sphere. Select the monkey. Go to the Shading buttons (F5).
Click the Ray Mirror button. Turn RayMir to 1. Then select the
UVSphere, go to the shading buttons, and turn on Ray Mirror, setting
it to 1. Press F12 to render. How about changing the mirror's

shape? Subdivide the plane, rotate a few vertices, and render. I'll
leave that to you.

As you can see, there are a lot of neat effects you can achieve with
Ray Mirror. I hope you have the basis for experimenting more and
getting the effect you desire. Happy Blendering!

Ambient Occlusion (2.5)

Watch the Video at: http://www.youtube.com/watch?v=rKUAemD7oo4

I have two goals for this video. The first goal is to familiarize you with the rendering settings of Blender 2.5. The second is to explain ambient occlusion, a powerful tool for rendering 3D objects more realistically. Even though I did this tutorial in 2.5, it should work in your version of Blender as well. Please note that this is based on a pre-alpha Windows version, as of September 15, 2009. As such, everything is subject to change. However, most probably, the basic user interface will not change that much. In addition, the renders can also change between this version and when Blender 2.5 officially is released, both because of implementation changes and tweaks to the algorithm.

We start with the default Blender 2.5 scene. The 3D window contains a camera, a lamp, and a cube, in perspective mode. Let's render the default scene. The scene icon, a camera, is where the settings for rendering the scene are set. The default dimensions are 1920 x 1080 pixels at 25% of full size, which gives a higher resolution image, with a lower size, than the old default of 800 x 600 pixels at 100%. The default output is Portable Network Graphics (.png), as opposed to JPEG. Here's the default Blender 2.5 scene.

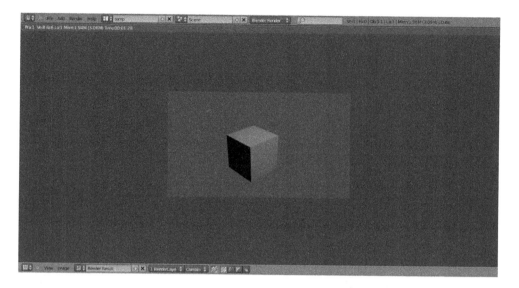

Note that the World colors have also changed, which explains the change in the cube's background.. The horizon colors are Red=.250, Green=.250 and Blue=.250. The old horizon colors were Red=.05, Blue=.22, Green=.40. The zenith colors are Red=.1, Green=.1, and Blue .1, and the ambient color is black (Red=0, Green=0, and Blue=0).

Let's add a plane to our scene, to show ambient occlusion. Remember to use SHIFT+A instead of the space bar to bring up the Add Object menu. Do SHIFT+A, Add Mesh, Plane. Position the plane below the cube by grabbing it (GKey) and relocating it below the cube. Then scale it 5 times with Right Click, followed by S, followed by 5, and pressing Enter. Now the cube lies above the plane. Press F12 to render. You should see the cube casting a shadow on the plane, as shown below.

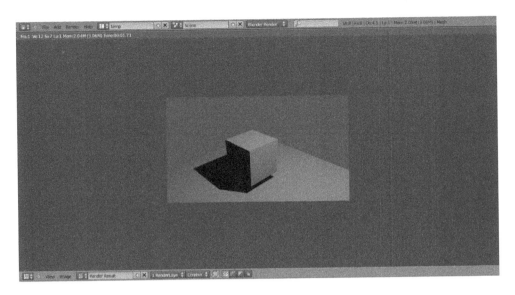

Now let's delete the lamp. Highlight the lamp (Right Click), press X (you can't use the DEL key), and confirm the delete. Now when we render, all the objects are black. The world colors render where there are no objects. The render should display as shown below.

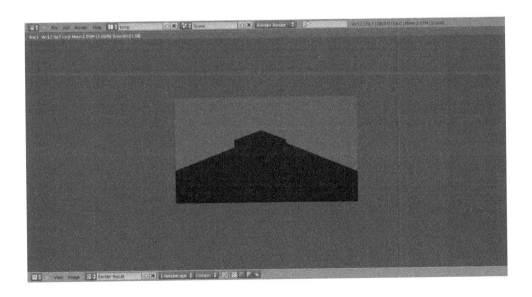

Ambient occlusion uses the ambient color, combined with a mathematical technique that darkens corners or areas hidden by other objects (the word "occlusion" is a fancy word for hidden). Lets go

to the World buttons and find the Ambient Occlusion panel. Check the
Ambient Occlusion check box, accept the defaults, and press F12 to
render. In the older versions of Blender, press F8 for the material
buttons, then the World subcontext, find the Amb Occ panel, and click
on Ambient Occlusion. Here's the render I got.

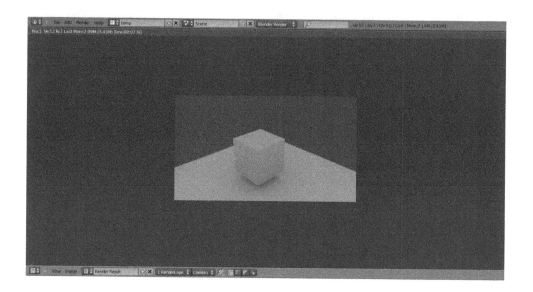

Blender uses the World colors to color the cube and the plane, and
then rendered a small shadow on the plane. The shadow is larger as
the cube moves closer to the plane.   Move the cube closer to the
plane, use the G key and move in the negative X direction. Then
press F12 to render.

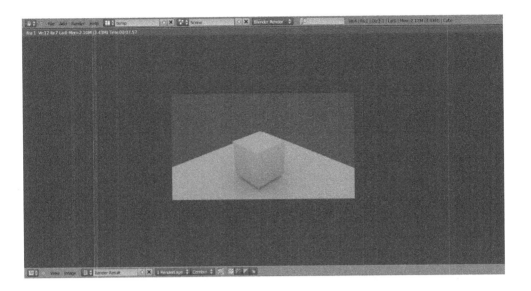

This render took about 7 seconds. If you raise the number of samples up to 10, the shadows become crisper, but the render time is much slower. This simple render took about 24 seconds - over 3 times slower.

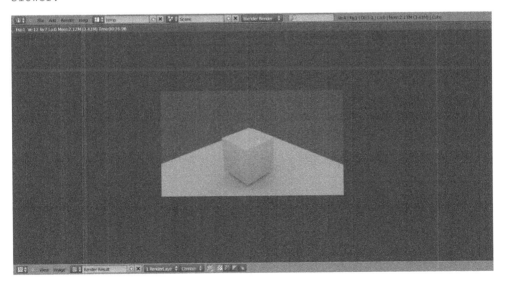

Set the samples back to 5.

By default, ambient occlusion uses ray tracing, casting rays from each pixel of each object. If the ray finds an object before reaching the World, the pixel is darkened. The resulting shadows are affected by the closeness of the object. Go to the World buttons. If you turn off all the Shading check boxes (they're all on by default), you won't get any ambient occlusion.

The two check boxes you need to check (buttons in earlier versions), are Shadows (to get any shadow effects at all), and Ray Tracing. Now if you render, with F12, you'll get AO (shorthand for Ambient Occlusion).

Approximate Ambient Occlusion is a way to get faster rendering with good AO effects, though not as good as ray traced AO. Turn off Ray Tracing (but keep Shadows on). Then go to the World buttons and click Approximate. Then render (F12). Here's the result on my computer.

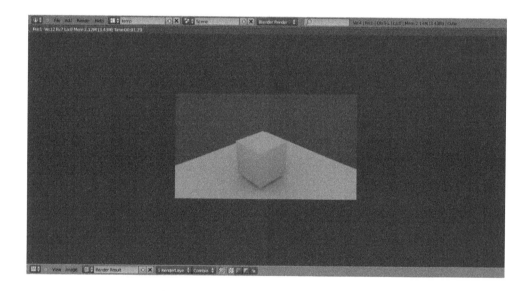

Not quite as precise an AO render, but the render time was less than 3 seconds. Approximate AO is a great choice for animation because of the tremendous savings in rendering time. Choose it while you're developing, and turn on ray tracing AO on the final render.

Add a UV Sphere and a monkey to to the scene, moving them close to the cube and slightly above the plane. Press F12 to render. You should see shadows cast by all three objects on each other.

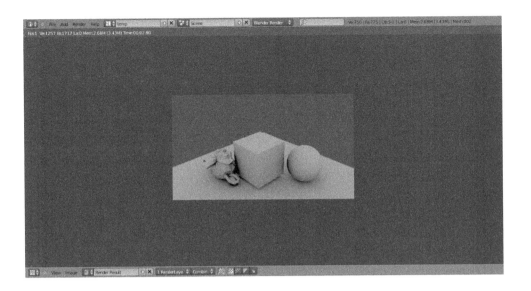

Here's an interesting effect. Change the horizon color to a nice
blue shade. Change the color to Sky Color from the default of White.
Press F12 to render.

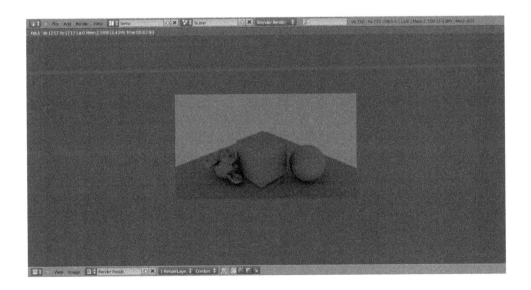

The scene is now affected by the sky color. This only scratches the
surface. You can play with the Falloff, Pixel Cache, Attenuation,
and other settings, as well as combine AO with the lamps in your

scene. I hope this gives you good ideas for making your scenes more realistic.

Radiosity (2.49)

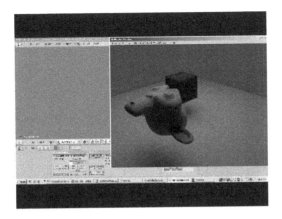

Watch the Video at: http://www.youtube.com/watch?v=_M4ffj2w_WY

Conventional lighting systems use lamps and cameras. The light is emitted from the lamps, bounces off the object, and then interacts with the camera to determine how the object is lit. The object is basically a passive receiver of light.

Radiosity takes a different approach. No lamps are necessary, although radiosity can be used to supplement traditional lamp based lighting. Instead, the objects themselves, or at least the ones you designate as light emitters, are the light source. They also receive light, but this time from other objects. This occurs in real life, and it's not limited to lamps. Think of lit matches, fire, glowing embers, or atomic bombs. Radiosity is a mathematical calculation of how objects that emit light interact with objects that receive light. Most objects actually do both at the same time. Radiosity rendering can produce stunning effects, but it takes getting used to. The goal of this tutorial is just to make you comfortable with radiosity setup.

Start by deleting the lamp. Radiosity does not need the lamp because the light comes from the materials applied to the objects. Right click on the lamp, and press X to confirm the delete.

Add a UV Sphere to the scene, with Space – Add – Mesh - UVSphere. We'll give the UVSphere 16 segments and 16 rings. The top half of the UV Sphere will be our light source, acting somewhat like a hemi lamp, with a soft hemispheric lighting effect and soft shadows. Move the UVSphere so that it is above the cube. Grab it, with the G key,

and move it up. Scale the UVSphere 5 times - S 5 then ENTER. Press
Z to go into wireframe mode and Tab to go into Edit mode.

We need to delete the bottom half. Press the A key to deselect the
vertices. Then box select (B key) all the bottom vertices. Press
the X key to delete the selected faces on the bottom half. We're
left with a hemisphere.

Press F5 for the Shading buttons, and click on the Material button.
Click Add New to add a material. Give the cube R, G, and B values
each of .5, so that the hemisphere will emit equal amounts of each.
Click on the Shaders panel, and set the Emit value to .02. It's a
small number, but the UVSphere has many faces which will generate
sufficient light for the scene.

We need to make sure that the normals are pointing towards the cube.
Light is emitted from the face normals. Press F9 to go to the Edit
buttons. In the Mesh Tools More panel, click on Draw Normals. Set
NSize to 1.0. Select all the vertices by pressing the A key. Note
that the normals are outside, so the light will not reach the cube.
To fix this, press the W key and select Flip Normals to have the face
normals point inward.

Before we continue, we need to make sure radiosity is enabled in our
render. Press F10 for the Scene buttons, turn on Radiosity, and turn
off SS, Ray, Shadow, and Envmap. The entire scene will be lit by the
UVSphere radiosity.

Let's set the camera as well. Set the scene so that the UVSphere is
providing hemispherical light to the cube, which is a bit off of the
plane. Move the hemisphere up a bit, out of the camera view. Move
the camera in a bit towards the cube.

Now we'll create a white ground plane from which the shadows will
fall. Tab out of Edit mode. Add a plane - Space-Add-Mesh-Plane,
and scale it 5 times - S 5 Enter. Grab it and move it below the cube
with some space between the bottom of the cube and the plane.

Press the Shading button (F5) and add a new material by clicking the
Add New button. Make the plane white by setting the R, G, and B
sliders all the way to 1. We need to make sure that the normals are
facing upward. Tab into Edit mode. In the Editing Context, Mesh
Tools More panel, click Draw Normals and set Normal Size to 1. The
normals point downward. They need to point upward. Press the W key
and select Flip Normals to fix this.

Tab out of Edit mode. Select the cube, Shift F2. Click the Shading button, F5. Set the material color to Blue, R=0, G=0, B=1. Tab into Edit Mode. We need to check the normals. From the Mesh Tools More panel, click Draw Normals and Set Normal Size to 1. Indeed, the normals face outside, which is correct. Tab out of Edit mode.

Now we're ready for our first radiosity render. Tab out of edit mode. Press the Radioactive icon, for radiosity. Before we start the calculation, press the Gour button, which is a good choice for radiosity with shadows. SHIFT+Select the cube, the plane, and the UV Sphere: every object in the scene except the camera. All of these will participate in the radiosity calculation. In the Radio Tools panel, click the Collect Meshes button. Now we're ready for the calculation. Click the big GO button for the radiosity calculation. I'll pause the video while the radiosity calculation does its thing. See you when it's done. Press F12 to render.

Next, we'll add a yellow monkey next to the cube. First, press the Free Radio Data button to clear the radiosity calculations. We are going to recalculate te radiosity after we add the monkey. Press Space, Add, Mesh, Monkey. Click the Shading Buttons, F5. Add a yellow material, by clicking the Add New, and setting Red to 1, Green=1, and Blue to 0. Note that Ambient is .5, which means that the monkey can receive 1/2 of the light sent to it from the UVSphere. Emit is 0. The monkey is only receiving light, not emitting it. Tab into Edit mode. Press F9 for the Edit windows. Note that the face normals are pointing outward, to receive the light, so we're fine.

Tab into object mode. Smooth the monkey by pressing the Set Smooth button. Then add a Subsurf modifier at Level 2.

Press F12 to render. I'll pause the video again until it's done.

This just scratches the surface. You get more realistic rendering if you work with more geometry. Experiment with the different settings that influence the radiosity calculation. You may want more defined shadows or a different color mix. You can also mix radiosity with other non-lamp lighting effects, such as ambient occlusion. Happy Blendering!

Rendering With YafaRay (2.49)

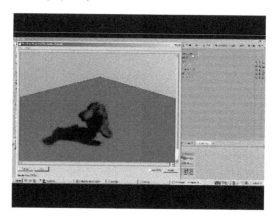

Watch the Video at: http://www.youtube.com/watch?v=YrPZPLNKVq8

YafaRay is an external renderer (download it from www.yafaray.org)
that is integrated with Blender 2.49 via Python scripts. You can add
many dramatic features, such as global illumination, caustics,
enhanced ray tracing, and self illuminated objects, to your renders,
with YafaRay. YafaRay extends Blender's built in renderer with
special types of lighting, new material options, and enhanced world
settings. It's not intuitive how to run YafaRay to get these
features. YafaRay works with the settings you set up in Blender,
ignores some of them, and adds other features. The goal of this
tutorial is to show you an efficient workflow of Blender and YafaRay.
I can't cover all of the features in a short video. Hopefully, there
will be enough for you to get started and to explore more on your
own. There's no substitute for practice. I am assuming that you
have installed YafaRay correctly to work with Blender 2.49b.

1) Delete the default cube. Go to Front View (NUM1). Add the
monkey (Space - Add - Mesh - Monkey). Give the monkey a red material
by going to the Shading buttons (F5) and clicking Add New. Set the
diffuse color to R=1, G=0 and B=0. Name the material MonkeyMat, so
we can track it in YafaRay. It's a good idea to name the material
something that is associated with the object it's with, to track it
in YafaRay. Go to the Edit buttons (F9). Press Set Smooth. Add a
plane below the monkey (Space - Add - Mesh - Plane). Scale the plane
up 10 times (S - 10 - ENTER). Add a green material by pressing F5
(Shading), selecting Add New, and setting the diffuse color to R=0,
G=1, and B=0. Name the material PlaneMat. Press F12 to render,
using the Blender internal renderer.

2) Split the 3D window into two, one on the left and the other on the right. Change the left window to a Scripts window. Change the right window to an Outline window. Click on the Scripts menu. Select the Render menu item. Then click YafaRay Export 0.1.1. Press the RENDER button to see how YafaRay renders the same scene. Everything looks grayish, including the background. Neither the monkey's material, the plane's material, nor the background, is applied in the render. The World background is not applied either.

3) Some Blender 3D settings are exported to YafaRay. Others are not. Let's fix the World setting first. To fix that, click on World. There are a number of background settings. For a single color, click on Single Color and select the color. Let's make it blue (R=0, G=0, B=1). Click RENDER. We now have a blue background.

4) We can also have a gradient. Close the render window. Click the World button again. Select Gradient. You can have a Horizon color, a Zenith color, a Horizon Ground color, and a Zenith Ground color. Click RENDER.

5 An intriguing World setting is Sun Sky, which gives a sunny background. Again, close the render window and click the World button. Click on Sun Sky. Click on the Add Real Sun button. Click RENDER. Now the world looks sunny. There are quite a number of options you can play with.

6) Let's fix the monkey and plane materials. Click the Always Show Active Object button so that we can be sure we're working on the material for the active object (PlaneMat for the Plane, MonkeyMat for the Monkey). Let's make the plane a green Shiny Diffuse material. Change the Color to Green (R=0, G=1, B=0). Press the RENDER button to see the change. In the Outline window, click on Suzanne to change the active object to the monkey. Make the monkey a Shiny Diffuse material as well. Change its color to Red (R=1, G=0, B=0). Press the RENDER button. Now the monkey is red, the plane is green, and the background is blue, similar to the render from Blender's internal renderer.

7) An interesting built in YafaRay material is Coated Glossy. Let's apply that material to Suzanne. Change the Diffuse color to Red, and the Glossy color to Yellow (R=1, G=1, B=0). Click the RENDER button. There are many other material settings you can play with.

8) The Blender camera has additional capabilities in YafaRay. Change the selected object to the Camera. Click the Objects button. The default mode is Perspective, as in Blender 3D. A dramatic effect is Angular, which gives us a spherical, angular look when we render.

We can adjust the Max angle to change the diameter of the sphere, giving the render a fisheye effect. The Mirrored effect gives the apparence of the scene as if from behind a mirror. Click the Mirrored button. You can adjust the mirror angle. Orthographic gives results similar to Blender's orthographic camera. Change the Scale to 15 and click the RENDER button. Architect is similar to orthographic, except that the vertical lines are parallel.

9) If you want to save the render as an image file, you need to do it before you exit out of the render window. Click the RENDER button. From the Image button, click Save As. YafaRay lets you save an image as a BMP file, a PNG file (which has an alpha channel), and an EXR file (for HDR images that include extra color information).

10) You can make any mesh a light source in YafaRay. The light emanates from the face normals of the mesh. To illustrate, let's make the monkey a mesh light. Select Suzanne from the outliner. Click on Object in YafaRay. Then click Enable meshlight, and press RENDER. Suzanne acts like a light bulb, even casting shadows of itself on the plane! Neat! Click Enable Meshlight again to turn off the monkey as a mesh light.

11) YafaRay adds more functionality to the different Blender lamps. From the Outline window, select the Lamp. In the Buttons window, change the Lamp type to Sun. Click the RENDER button. The Sun lamp, when turned on, gives the effect of direct sunlight. The light can project either as a cylinder or a cone.

12) From the Buttons window, change the lamp to a Spot light. In YafaRay, change the type to Spot. Click the RENDER button. Now we have a nice spot light. We can adjust the Spot Size (angle) and the blurriness of the spot in the buttons window, in Blender 3D itself.

13) Go to 3D view. Let's duplicate the lamp, move it to the left side of the monkey, and rotate the lamp to point at the monkey. Change the lamp to an area lamp. Go back to YafaRay by selecting Yafaray Export 0.1.1 from the Render menu. Click the RENDER button. Now you have shadows coming from the area and sot lamps.

14) Click on Settings. You can turn on Ambient Occlusion under the Direct Lighting settings, with AO type shadows. You can also try Photon Mapping, which produces the results you see. Path Tracing gives you yet another option to customize your render.

I hope this gives you some idea of the power of the combination of Blender and YafaRay. It's a great combination. There's certainly more you can explore.

Materials and Textures

Bump Map Texture (2.49)

Watch the Video at: http://www.youtube.com/watch?v=o_blkxlZSqA

Many times, simply mapping an image texture does not highlight the detail of the image enough. Blender's bump map is one of the ways that you can make the images in your scene more exciting and realistic. The goal of this video is to show how bump maps do this. In keeping with the October Halloween mood, we'll start with a jpeg image of pumpkins. These pumpkins, like most, have a lot of deep indentations, and other imperfections. In the 3D world, imperfections are good because they make the scene more realistic. Think of an orange peel. What's more realistic, a peel that's orange everywhere, or one where all the ridges and dimples of the orange show? It's the same with pumpkins.

A bump map is a mathematical calculation of each pixel's height, based on an image. The bump map texture is independent of the underlying mesh. This makes bump mapping far easier than trying to simulate the height effects by adding more geometry to your mesh. Think of adding vertices and faces at every place in an orange peel mesh where you want some height or depth.

OK, let's get started.

1) Delete the default cube, with Right click to select, then X, then Enter to confirm.

2) Add a plane, with Space-Add-Mesh-Plane. Scale it up 10 times (S 10 ENTER).

3) Split the 3D view in half. Make the right half a UV/Image Editor window.

4) In the UV/Image Editor window, from the Image Editor, open the Pumpkins.jpg image. At http://blender3dvideos.blogspot.com, I have a link to the image I used. You can either use that one, or load any image you want. Select the Image and click Open Image.

5) In the 3D window on the left, from the View Menu, select Align View, then Align Active Camera To View, or press CTRL+NUM0.

6) From the Buttons window, press F10 for the Scene buttons. At the bottom left corner is where you can select where the render output will display. The default is a separate window. Change it to Image Editor. This will let us compare the reference image with the image with our adjustments applied.

7) Select the plane (right click). Add a material, by pressing F5 (Shading), then the Material purple sphere, then click Add New.

8) We're going to select a color from our reference image as our base color. Later, we'll change it to see different effects. Click the Color rectangle, then the Sample button. Go to the reference image in the UV/Image Editor window, and select an orange color that will serve as the background color for the rendered image.

9) Press F12 to render. The plane is orange, but there's a big white spot on the upper right corner of it. This is the result of specular highlights. We want to turn this off. Click on the Shaders tab, find the Spec slider, and turn it to 0. Press F12 to render. Now the specular highlights are gone.

10) Press F6 for the texture buttons. Click Add New. Click on Image. Select Image as the Texture Type. Click on the Load button. Load the Pumpkins.jpg image. Press F12 to render. The pumpkin jpeg is now on the plane.

11) To make the image a bump map, click on the Material buttons. Go
to the Map To panel, all the way on the right. We'll make a full
bump map. Turn off Col, for Color, and turn on Nor, for Normal.
Increase the Normal slider to 20, to make the effect obvious. Press
F12 to render. As you can see, the pumpkins look more realistic than
before, but we don't have any color.

12) Turn on the Col button, and press F12. Now the orange pumpkin
color is back without affecting the bump map.

There are many other artistic type effects you can do. Here's an
example. Go to the Texture buttons, F6. Change XRepeat to 4 and
YRepeat to 4. This makes the image repeat. The bump map effect
repeats as well.

Any time you want to save a render, press F3. You can use the JPEG
somewhere else, say as part of a Halloween party invitation. I think
you'll agree that this is much easier than creating a mesh that looks
like these pumpkins. I hope this gives you some ideas about how to
use bump maps to make your Blender scenes more realistic.

Multiple Materials (2.49)

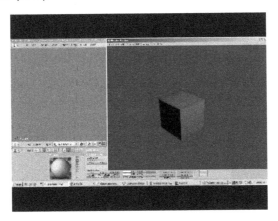

Watch the Video at: http://www.youtube.com/watch?v=hCYViRJFf5w

Many times you will be assigning one material to an entire object.
However, there are situations where you want to assign different
parts of an object to their own material. The assignment can get
kind of tricky. In this demo, we will make each face of a cube have
a different colored material. You can then extend this to customize
each material, such as changing its opacity or transparency, on each
face. You can also add separate textures to each material. This
tutorial shows you how to do the first step: creating a separate
material for each face of a cube.

Steps:
1) We'll start with the default 2.49b scene and use the default
cube. Press Tab to go to Edit mode. Go to Face Select mode (Control
- Tab - 3 or the triangle icon. Press A to deselect all faces.
Rotate the cube on its side, to make selecting a face easier. Press
Z to go to wireframe mode.

Materials are assigned per face. Each face can have only 1 material
ID. New materials are given the next material ID, 2 for the second
one, 3 for the third one, and so on. A set of buttons in Edit (F9(
assigns multiple material IDs. By default, when you Add New
material, all faces have a Material ID 1. Press F5 for the shading
buttons. There's an indicator (1 Mat 1) that shows how many
materials are on the object (1), and which one we're working on (1).

2) Create 5 new materials. By default, each face of the cube has a
material, called Material, assigned to it. The Material button group

shows that there is 1 material assigned to the cube. Press F9 to get to the Editing buttons. Press the New key 5 times. Now there are 6 materials, with the names Material, Material.001, Material.002, all the way to Material.005.

3) Assign the faces to their respective materials:

Go to F9 (Editing buttons). Assign the faces as follows:

Select the top face. Set its material to Material (ID = 1). Click Assign.

Select the bottom face. Set its material to Material.001 (ID = 2). Click Assign.

Select the left face. Set its material to Material.002 (ID = 3) Click Assign.

Select the right face. Set its material to Material.003 (ID=4). Click Assign.

Select the front face. Set its material to Material.004 (ID = 5). Click Assign.

Select the back face. Set its material to Material.005 (ID=6). Click Assign.

You can verify which material is associated with which face. Press the A key to deselect all faces. Select a material, say Material.004. Click the Select button and you should see that the material is assigned to the top face. You can also do the opposite. Press A to deselect all faces. Click the bottom face. Click the question mark icon. You should see that Material.001, with material ID 2, is assigned.

4) Click F5 to go to the Shading buttons. We want our materials to have meaningful names so we can identify them easily. Assign the following colors:

Material: Red (R=1, G=0, B=0). Press Autoname to have Blender create a meaningful name (Red).

Material.001: Green (R=0, G=1, B=0). Press Autoname. Blender calls this LightGreen.

Material.002: Blue (R=0, G=0, B=1). Press Autoname. Blender calls this LightBlue.

Material.003: Yellow (R=1, G=1, B=0). Press Autoname. Blender calls this material Yellow.

Material.004: Magenta (R=1, G=0, B=1). Press Autoname. Blender calls this material Magenta.

Material.005: Cyan (R=0, G=1, B=1). Press Autoname. Blender calls this material Cyan.

To view our result, press Tab to go into Object mode. Then go into Shaded mode. Rotate the cube. Press F12 to render.

You can further refine this by changing the characteristics of a material by playing with settings such as Ray Mirror, Alpha, Ray Transparency, the render pipeline, and so on. You can produce some interesting effects.

Animated Procedural Textures (2.49)

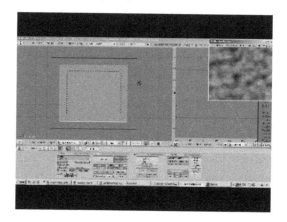

Watch the Video at: http://www.youtube.com/watch?v=3DD1SRipFXs

You might get the idea that location, rotation, and scale are the
only things you can animate. In fact, there are many other areas in
which you can animate. In this tutorial, I will show how to animate
a procedural texture to create a wavelike or moving cloud effect.
This technique is based on the excellent series of tutorials by Colin
Litster, at www.cogfilms.com. If you really want to create a
realistic ocean effect, make clouds float by realistically, make a
flag wave, and so on, you should check out all of Colin's tutorials.
This techniques has become very popular in the Blender community.
Colin been a driving force in the Blender community for a long time.

Blender's textures come in two forms, procedural and image. If
you've worked with Blender for even a short time, you've probably
encountered the Image texture, which is simply the projection of a 2D
image into an object, such as a plane. Image textures are non-
procedural. The image, what you see, is what you get. Procedural
textures are really little programs that you can tweak to get a
particular special effect. One of the most commonly used procedural
texture is Clouds. We're going to animate the Clouds procedural
texture, projected onto a colorless, shadeless plane, to produce a
wavelike effect.

You can download the blend file that I created, that you can use in
your own projects and share freely. You can find the link at my
blog, http://blender3dvideos.blogspot.com, where you can also read
the script for my tutorial, as well as the scripts for all the
tutorials I've published.

So start with the default Blender scene. Delete the default cube
(Right click to select, press the DEL key, then Enter to confirm).
Add a plane (Space - Add - Mesh - Plene). Scale it 3 times (S - 3 -
Enter). Orient the camera so that it faces the plane (View - Align
View - Align Active Camera to View, or press CTRL - Alt - Num 0).
Scale the plane in the X and Y direction so that it fills out the
outer dashed line rectangle. This will ensure that the camera sees
the entire plane, without the background rendering.

Press the Shading button (F5) and use the default material
(Material). Press F12 to render. The plane renders with the default
gray color and the specular highlight. We're going to make the
animated procedural texture control both the shape and the color of
the rendered plane. To get rid of the specular highlight, click the
Shadelees button. Press F12 to render. In the Map To panel, all the
way at the right, make the color black.

Press F6 or click on the icon next to the ball to go to the Texture
buttons. The first texture channel (channel 0, technically, we need
to remember that), with the word Tex is selected. The texture we
select will be mapped to that channel. There are 10 texture slots.
We can blend all sorts of textures (images, clouds, blending types,
and so on) using these slots. We'll use the default Channel 0. From
the Texture Type dropdown, choose Clouds. You can control how the
clouds look using the sliders and the various types of noise, such as
soft noise or hard noise. Accept the defaults. You can play with
these later to get the effect you want.

Press F12 to render. You get a sort of black and white wavy picture
produced by the clouds texture. We are now going to animate this so
that it looks like real waves. Split the 3D view. From the bottom
border of the window, right click when you see the double arrows.
Select Split Area. Move the cursor to where you want the view to be
split. Press Enter. Then change the type of the newly created
window at the right to IPO Curve Editor.

We're going to work with the IPO Curve Editor in full screen mode.
To do that, position the cursor inside the editor area and press
CTRL+Down Arrow. The IPO Type is set t Object by default. There are
other types that can be set. Change the IPO Type to Material. Note
on the right all the different things that can be changed - red,
green, and blue channels, the alpha (for transparency), specularity,
hardness, and so on.

We're going to change two offsets, the X offset (OfsX) and the Z
offset (OfsZ). The X offset controls the track of the texture across
the Z axis, making it seem to move across the window. The Z offset
changes the shape of the cloud/wave texture. We'll animate this over

100 frames. Start with OfsX. Left click OfsX. Zoom the view using
the Num+ and Num-, so that you can see the 1 and -1 values on the
right. These represent the number of Blender units to offset as the
animation proceeds. At about Frame 1 (it's not necessary to be
totally exact), with the value at -1, press CTRL+LMB. A horizontal
curve is created. Go to Frame 100 or so. CTRL+LMB where the value
is 1.

You now created a Bezier curve interpolated between those two values,
for the 100 frames. To make the curve interpolate linearly, go to
the Curve menu, then select Interpolation, then Linear. We can
extrapolate this line both forward and backward in time by selecting
Curve - Extend Mode - Extrapolation.

We'll do the opposite for OfsZ, going from 1 to -1. SHIFT+LMB OfsZ
at the right. At Frame 1, find the value of 1, and press CTRL+LMB.
Then go to Frame 100. Find the value of -1, and press CTRL+LMB.
Then go to the curve menu and change the interpolation to linear.
Finally, from the Curve Menu, we'll change Extend Mode to
Extrapolation. We now have our two curves created.

Press CTRL+Down Arrow to return the IPO Curves Editor back to its
original position. We can't see the animation effect in the texture
with ALT+A. We need to actually animate the scene. To do that, go
to the Scene buttons by pressing F10. Change the end frame to 100.
Select the Preview preset by pressing the Preview button, all the way
at the right. Just for this demo, we'll animate this as a series of
JPEGs. You can create a video out of this by selecting AVI or MOV
format. So press the ANIM button to animate. Looks sort of wavy,
doesn't it?

We can make it a bit more realistically water looking. To do that,
select the Material buttons, go to the Map To panel, and change the
color to something bluish. Press F10 to go back to the scene
buttons. Then press ANIM.

That's it! You're now an animated procedural texture guru. You
might also tweak the clouds setting, especially the noise type and
amount, or try some of Blender's other procedural textures.

UV Unwrapping An Image (2.49)

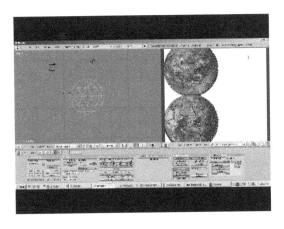

Watch the Video at: http://www.youtube.com/watch?v=I_8OV92HLPY

The purpose of this tutorial is to show how to unwrap a globe into two hemispheres. This tutorial is based on the UV Map Basics Tutorial, in the Blender 3D: Noob To Pro Wikibook, at http://en.wikibooks.org/wiki/Blender_3D:_Noob_to_Pro/UV_Map_Basics. The URL is in the Youtube notes, as well as at blender3dvideos.blogspot.com, the Web site for my tutorials.

Why do we need this tutorial? The reason: UV Mapping was introduced way back in Blender 2.34 and has been extensively rewritten since then. The user interface, and many terms, have changed over time. As examples, UV Face Select mode disappeared in Blender 2.46, and the term LSCM (Least Squares Conformal Mapping) was used up until then. Now LSCM is simply called Unwrap. Many unwrapping tutorials were based on earlier versions. If you try to follow along in the current version, 2.49b, you can get confused. Hopefully, this video will help to show the steps to successful UV Unwrapping in the version most of us use.

So let's get started. Here's the default scene in Blender 2.49b. Delete the default cube (right click, then press X and confirm the delete). Add an icosphere (Space - Add - Mesh - Icosphere), accepting the default of 2 subdivisions. Scale it 3 times (S 3) to make a large globe. Let's smooth the globe out. From the Editing buttons (F9), press Set Smooth. Then add a subsurf modifier at level 2.

Split the 3d viewport horizontally, by clicking on the border, right click, select Split, positioning the vertical line to where the split should be, and pressing Enter. Make the left window a UV /Image Editor window.

Click on the border of the User Preferences window and drag down to show the user preferences. Click View Name so we can see the view name (Top Ortho). Then click on the border and drag up to free up the area for the 3D view.

Tab into edit mode, and press the A key to deselect all vertices. We're going to make a seam for the UV editor to split the sphere in two parts. To do that, press Num3 to go into side view (right ortho). We're going to box select the vertices at the equator so that when the sphere is unwrapped, the UV unwrap program will know how to split the sphere. So box select (Bkey) the vertices at the equator and press Enter. Press CTRL+E, which brings up the Edge Specials menu, and select Mark Seam.

Press the A key to deselect the seam and the A key again to select all vertices. Press the U key, which brings up the UV Calculation menu. Select Unwrap. This is actually LSCM Unwrap masquerading under a simpler name. There are many other ways to UV unwrap an object, as you can see. The sphere is unwrapped in the UV/Image Editor window.

The easiest way to actually place the image onto the sphere is to export the unwrapping map to an image editor, such as Photoshop or the Gimp. I use the Gimp, but Photoshop will work just as well. To do this, from the UVs menu item, select Scripts, and choose Save UV Face Layout. Accept the default of 512 x 512 pixel map, which is perfect both for non Game and Game use in Blender, and save the file (it's a Targa image file) in your project directory.

Now open up the Gimp. Here are the steps I found that seemed to work well. First, open up the saved file we just created. Then open up the image to apply to the sphere. You can download the globe hemisphere image, BlueMarble 2001-2002.jpg from the UV tutorial wiki page. Go to the targa file first and find the diameter of the spheres that we need to fit the image to. The diameter is 270 pixels.

Switch to the BlueMarble jpg, the one containing the two globes. Choose the Ellipse Select tool and turn on the Fixed Aspect Ratio check box to make sure that we will do a circle select. Select the left globe. Copy (CTRL+C) the globe to the clipboard. Switch to the reference file. From the Edit Menu, select Paste As, and choose New

Layer. Press Enter to confirm. Click on the Move tool (the one with the cross hairs) and move the globe to the center of the top series of triangles.

From the Layer menu, select Scale. Enter 272. I like to go a pixel a two more than the actual diameter to make sure we don't get any background artifacts included. Press Scale and position the expanded globe over the layout if necessary.

Now go back to the bluemarble jpg and choose the Circle Select tool. First Select None, to deselect the left globe. This time, circle select the right globe. Copy (CTRL+C) the globe to the clipboard. Switch to the reference file. From the Edit Menu, select Paste As, and choose New Layer. Choose the Move tool and move the globe to the center of the bottom set of triangles. From the Layer Menu, choose Scale, and scale the globe to 272 pixels as well.

Press CTRL+L to bring up the Layers menu. There are 3 layers, the original reference image and the two globe layers. Deselect the original reference image by clicking on the eye. Close the Layers menu. We now can save our file - we'll make it a jpeg - which will be just the two hemispheres. We'll call it FinalGlobe.jpg. Accept the Flatten Image dialog because that's what we want. Click on Export and accept the defaults.

Now go back to Blender. From the Image menu, open the FinalGlobe jpg. You might need to make some last minute tweaks to eliminate some dark background artifacts. Press the Shading buttons (F5). Add a new material. Click the TexFace button to tell the renderer to use the Unwrapped UVs. Press F12 to render. From here, you might need to add a lamp. If you go into Texture mode you can see the image on the sphere.

That's it. I hope this gives you the basics of UV unwrapping a globe image and gives you some ideas for its use. If you want to create games and need images, this is essential because Blender's game engine requires UV textured images. Happy Blendering.

UV / Image Editor Basics (2.49)

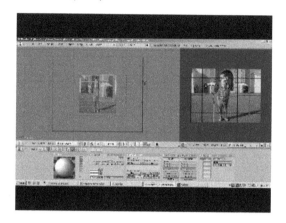

Watch the Video at: http://www.youtube.com/watch?v=JTK2C7twwUg

The purpose of this video is to show how to edit an image in the UV /
Image Editor in Blender 2.49b. Editing an image with the UV / Image
Editor is important when you're combining (the technical word is
"compositing") images and objects into a final render, as well as for
creating custom textures. The process involves mapping a 3D surface
onto one or many 2D images, a process called UV unwrapping a mesh.
The mapping is done on each face. It's possible for each mesh face
to have its own image mapped to it. We'll start with the simplest
case of UV unwrapping, unwrapping an image onto a plane, which has,
of course, only one face. We'll work our way up from there.

1) Erase the default cube (right click on the cube, then press the
DEL key, then Enter). Add a plane (Space - Add - Mesh - Plane).
Scale it up 3 times (S - 3 - Enter). Split the window horizontally
by right clicking on the 3D Window bottom border, choosing Split
Area, and positioning the double arrows so that the window is split.

2) We're going to play with a picture of me, in front of one of the
26 palaces of the King of Morocco, in Rabat, Morocco, projected onto
a plane. It's good to be the king. Select the plane. Tab into Edit
Mode. Press the A key twice to make sure that all the vertices are
selected. Press the U key to unwrap the plane. Choose the default
Unwrap method. The result: after you unwrap the plane, in the UV /
Image Editor you should see a square with 4 vertices - actually, it's
a face.

3) The next step is to load my image. From the UV / Image Editor,
select Image, then Open. Select the Image. You might need to use

the Zoom In and Zoom Out keys (NUM+ or NUM-) to position the image so that it fills up the square. There's the picture. In the background are soldiers, in their typical position before the Moroccan Changing Of The Guard.

4) The next step is to get my picture to display, both on the plane in the 3D view, and in rendering the image. We want the camera to see the image projected on a flat plane. To do that, from the View menu, press Align View, then Align Active Camera to View, or press CTRL+ALT+NUM0. Press F12 to render. The plane renders right now with the default gray material.

5) To get my picture to render, we need to tell the renderer to use the texture face (TexFace), which is the image from the UV / Image Editor. To do that, go to the Shading buttons (F5), select the default material (Material). Then, turn on the TexFace button. Now Press F12 to render. A bit better, but the image is upside down. We'll fix this shortly.

6) To see my image on the plane, go to View Properties. Turn on the SolidTex button. If the image still doesn't display, make sure the 3D View is in Solid mode. Now you can see me, upside down, as in the render. How can we fix this? In one of two ways...either by rotating the image in the 3D view or rotating the image in the UV / Image Editor. We're not going to change the geometry in the 3D view. We'll fix it in the UV / Image Editor. To do that, with all the vertices selected, press the R key, then rotate it 180 degrees. You can hold the control key down when you're close to 180 (you can see the rotation at the bottom of the UV / Image editor). That way you get exactly 180 degrees.

Press Enter and the image is now correct, both in the 3D view and the UV / Image Editor.

7) The entire image doesn't have to be mapped to the plane. To show that, go to the UV / Image Editor, with all the vertices selected. Press the S key to scale. Reduce the square to a rectangle syhowing only part of the image. I'm scaling the square down to a rectangle which focuses more on me than on the palace. The square is now a tall rectangle. Press F12 to render. Gee, I gained some weight. Moroccan food can be fattening, I guess.

8) The reason for the weird result is that, although the plane starts out mapped to a square area on the image, when I scaled it down, it became wrapped to the rectangle. The rendering stretched my stomach out, to fill in the plane's square area. That is the problem with UV unwrapping. Each face is mapped in its own way to an area of the image. The way that you unwrap a mesh makes a big difference. I'm

going to show you how it can get even more weird. Press CTRL+Z to undo the edit. That's the fastest diet on record.

9) We can do much finer edits, simply by adding more faces to the plane. To do this, position the cursor inside the 3D view. Press the W key to bring up the Specials menu. Select Subdivide Multi. Make the number of cuts 5. Of course, it can be any number you want. This gives us a 6 x 6 grid, with 36 faces in total. Go into Face Select mode by clicking on the triangle icon. Press the A key to deselect everything. Select a face in the 3D view. In the UV / Image editor, you see both the loaded image, and the part of the image that is mapped to that particular face.

10) Let's see what those guards are really doing. Easy enough. Select the faces that map to the part of the image where the guards are. Press the S key to scale them up a bit. Press F12 to render. They have really neat uniforms, don't they?

11) We can also edit from the UV / Image Editor. Position the 3D cursor in the UV / Image Editor. Box Select the area mapped to my shoulder. Press the R key to rotate it a bit. Now I'm bending my body in a strange way. Press F12 to render.

12) To show you why the projection method makes a difference, I'm going to unwrap the plane based on the Sphere from View projection. The result is as if both me and the King's palace were put through a blender which, in a sense they were. Thank God for CTRL+Z.

You should play with all the different projection methods in Blender. A cube projection of an image actually will work fine. You can unwrap it and then scale the UV squares to fit the image. You can unwrap as many times as you like. Each unwrap undoes the previous one. However, you can have multiple unwraps if you want. The way to do that is to create a new texture map. The default name is UVTex. Click New and unwrap - the default name is UVTex.001, which you can change - and you can experiment with different unwrappings.

I hope this gives you a start in using the UV / Image Editor. Be sure to hit the Youtube Subscribe button so you won't miss any of my tutorials. Happy Blendering.

Color Picker (2.49)

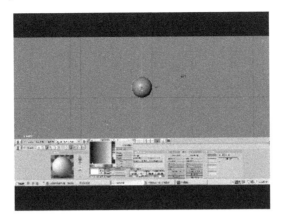

Watch the Video at: http://www.youtube.com/watch?v=Q7SQHbXjW6Y

The name of this Blender video tutorial is "Using The Blender 3D 2.49a Color Picker". I wrote this tutorial using Blender 2.49a.

If you've used any imaging software such as Photoshop, you're probably familiar with selecting a color using the RGB sliders. Of course, you can do this in Blender as well. However, there is a feature called the Color Picker which gives you a number of other ways of choosing colors. Anywhere Blender asks you for a color, you can use the color picker.

We start by firing up Blender with its default scene. We're going to delete the default cube (right click to select, then X or the DEL key to delete), and add a UV Sphere (Space - Add - Mesh - UVSphere). The standard way of selecting a color is to use the RGB sliders. We'll add a Material by selecting the UVSphere (Right Click) in Object Mode. To add a material, click the F5 (Shading) button, then the Materials button. Go to solid mode (press the Z key if you are in wireframe mode) so we can see the color. Then click the Add New button. To make the material red, drag the R slider all the way up to 1 and the G and B sliders all the way down to 0.

Another way to choose a color is by the combination of Hue, Saturation, and Value, or HSV. The color picker lets you do this either visually or by using the sliders in a similar fashion as RGB.

The rectangle to the left of the Col text has turned red to show the UVSphere's color. Left click on it to bring up the Color Picker.

Drag the little circle on the color picker swatch to change the hue. Dragging to the right increases the hue value from 0 to 1. Dragging to the left decreases the hue value from 1 to 0. As you drag, notice that the Hue settings, on the right, change as well.

There are two boxes, in the lower right part of the color picker. The lower box shows the old color. The box on top of it shows the new color. The color hasn't been applied yet. There are two ways to apply the color. You can drag the cursor out of the color picker box, or you can press Enter. In either case, the color is applied and the new color shows in the color rectangle.

Click on the color rectangle to bring up the color picker. You can also drag the little circle in the Saturation and Value square. The saturation ranges from 0 to 1 along the y axis, and the value ranges from 0 to 1 along the x axis. Note how the saturation and value sliders change as you move the circle. Drag the cursor out of the color picker into the 3D viewport to select the color.

Click on the color rectangle to bring up the color picker. There's another way to choose a color, by direct entry of a hexadecimal RGB value. Each RGB value can range from 0 to 255, which is 00 to FF in hexadecimal. Here's a cream color, for example, with a hexadecimal value of FFCC99. We can enter this value in the hexadecimal value area. Again, we drag the cursor out of the color picker into the 3D viewport to select the color.

Click on the color rectangle to bring up the color picker again. There are 16 presets which let you store custom colors in the color picker. You can select a color by clicking on one of the presets. Or, you can create your own preset, which Blender saves between sessions. That way, you can create your own palette. we'll create a color and then select a preset rectangle, then CTRL+LMB to create our custom preset.

Finally, the Sample button lets you select a color from anywhere within your Blender screen. After you press the Sample button the cursor turns into an eyedropper. Move the eyedropper anywhere within Blender and then left click to select the color that way.

You can use the Sample button, combined with the Image Browser, to sample a color from an image on your hard drive. Split the screen (position the cursor on the border, then right click and select Split), choose the Image Browser. Navigate to the directory containing your images. Then go back into the Color Picker, click the Sample button, and sample an image from the thumbnails shown on the Image Browser.

Blender's color picker gives you a number of ways of choosing colors beyond using the RGB sliders. You can select from the hue swatches, from the Saturation and Value square, or enter the HSV values

directly into the color picker. You can enter hexadecimal RGB value.
Or you can sample a color by pressing the Sample button.

Color Gradient Overlay (2.49)

Watch the Video at: http://www.youtube.com/watch?v=4nSriFcd9Fo

A slick effect that you can do in photo image editors such as
Photoshop or the GIMP is to overlay two or more images, so that one
image overlays another, creating a layered effect. You can do this
in Blender as well. The more you can do in Blender, the better,
because it saves the time and effort of switching from one program to
another.

We're going to combine the official photo of President Obama with the
official White House photo, so that the White House is the background
under President Obama's photo. Here's the goal. Using some nifty
texturing techniques in Blender, including Blender's own Blend
texture, we can achieve this effect with little effort.

We start by firing up Blender, with its default 2.49a startup scene. We're going to create a plane on which we will work with the images, so the first step is to delete the default cube. Highlight it by moving the cursor over the cube, then right click, and delete (pressing X or the DEL key).

Then we add a plane (Space - Add - Mesh - Plane) to the scene. Then we scale the plane up three times its original size (S 3), to get a space large enough to display the image properly. We then go to the Buttons window, select F5 (Shading), then the Material sub context button, then press the Add New button to add a material. Then we hit the Texture button (F6) to add a new texture. Then we go to texture Type, and select the Image type. All the way to the right, you'll see the Load button, which lets us load an image.

We're going to load the White House jpeg, the official White House image, as the background texture. Select the file, its name is filled into the file name area. Then press the LOAD IMAGE button.

The image is loaded into the Preview area. Press F12 to render the scene. The image is rendered on the plane, but we would like the image to be facing us, instead of being tilted. The simplest way of doing this is to go to the View menu, selecting Align View, and then Align Active Camera To View. Now when we press F12 to render, the White House image is facing the camera. However, we would also like the image to completely fill the camera area.

To do that, switch to Camera View (NUM0), select the plane (Right click), and scale it (S key) to fit the camera. Now the White House image fills the screen.

We go back to the Texture panel and rename this texture Whitehouse. When Blender renders, it starts with any materials on the object. Then, it renders each texture, starting with the topmost and proceeding on down. We're going to add President Obama's image on the third texture layer, skipping the second for the time being. You'll see why shortly.

Highlight the third rectangle down. Press the Add New button. Select the Image Type, then the Load button (at the right), and then select the Obama jpeg. Then press the Load Image button to load the image.

Press F12 to render. President Obama's image is rendered, replacing the White House. That's because Blender renders textures from the highest to the lowest placement. Internally, the White House image was rendered, but it was replaced by President Obama's. How do we show the White House in the background?

The answer: set up a Blend texture as the second one, between the White House and the President. This intermediate texture, which we label Blend, is one of Blender's built in textures. It was set up exactly for this situation, to blend textures - in this case our two images - together.

The Blend texture has two additional tabs - a Colors tab, and a Blend tab. The Colors tab controls the how the blend colors and opacity interact with the textures above and below. We select the Colors tab, and then click on the Colorband button. Note how the preview panel changes to a color gradient, from black to light blue. There are two "swatches", initially, numbered 0 and 1. The dashed line displays visually which swatch is selected, and its position on the gradient (from 0 on the extreme left to 1 on the extreme right) is selected. Swatch 0 is current - you can see that as well in the Cur: area. The color is black, with the R, G, and B settings at 0. Note that the A setting is 0. The A stands for the "alpha channel", which is the transparency setting. A value of 0 means totally transparent, which means that the white house image shows completely through.

Switching to swatch 1, the color setting is light blue (R=0, G=1, B=1) and the transparency is 1, which means that none of the white house image shows through. The gradient is set up so that as the image goes to the left, less of the White House and more of the President shows. You can play with adding gradients, changing the color and alpha settings, to get other effects. You can also play with the Blend tabs, currently set to LIN or linear. to get nice effects such as halo and diagonal gradients.

When we press F12 to render, we still see the President's image. There's still another step that we need to do. Go to the Materials panel. There is a panel way out on the right, with Texture, Map Input, and Map To tabs. This panel fine tunes the texture rendering. Select the Map To tab, all the way to the right. Press the Stencil button, the first one on the third row. Also, press the NORGB button.

Now press F12. We'll see the blended image result that we want.

One other problem: there's a big shiny bright spot on the image. This is due to the setting of the lamp. To fix it, select the lamp and activate the No Specular button. Press F12 to render, and the bright spot will be gone.

We've only scratched the surface. There are many neat imaging tricks you can accomplish in Blender with the Blend texture. Happy Blendering!

Animation

Animated 3D Text (2.49)

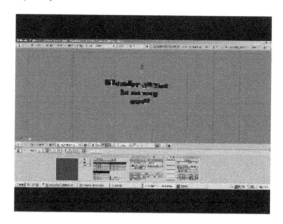

Watch the Video at: http://www.youtube.com/watch?v=1pmkpiIctOM

In this tutorial, I will show you how to create animated 3D text in Blender 2.49b. You can use this type of effect to create, for example, rolling credits in your video. Or, perhaps, you can do something like the Star Wars introduction..."A long, long time ago, in a galaxy far away...".

The techniques are based on Paolo Ciccone's excellent Blender 3D Survival Guide, which you can find at CreativeCow. Specifically, you can find how Paolo creates animated 3D text in Parts 3 and 4. The URLs are at:

http://library.creativecow.net/articles/ciccone_paolo/blender-survival-guide-3.php

http://library.creativecow.net/articles/ciccone_paolo/blender-survival-guide-4.php

You should watch Paolo's tutorials as well, because he discusses many other features of 3D text animation, such as lighting and camera positioning. Blender has so many features that it's impossible to cover all of them in one or two videos. The purpose of this tutorial is to show you the basic steps, a recipe for doing animated 3D text in Blender.

Here's the recipe:

1) Delete the default cube (right click, X to delete, Enter to confirm).

2) If you click inside the 3D window, the 3D cursor goes to the place where you click. That's the place where the next object will be created. We want the text to be placed at the origin, X=0, Y=0, and Z=0. To do that, there's a simple shortcut to place the 3D cursor there. Press SHIFT+C.

3) Create a new Text object (Space - Add - Text). The text object has the word Text, placed on the floor. The text object is actually a curve object.

4) Press Tab to go into Edit mode. For a text object, when you press the Tab key, you can change the text. There is a cursor, a vertical bar. Let's change the text so that it says "Blender 3D text is so very cool!" on 3 lines. Press the backspace key 4 times to remove the word Text. Then type "Blender 3d text". Press Enter to go to the next line. Then type "is so very". Press Enter to go to the next line. Type "cool!". Press Tab to go back to Object Mode.

5) Let's make the camera see the text, in the view. From the View menu, select Align View, then Align Active Camera to View. Alternatively, you could have pressed CTRL+ALT+Num0. Now the 3D view is in camera view. Rotate the text 30 degrees in the Y direction (R Y 30). Press the Scale key to scale the text up 1.5 times (S 1.5 Enter). Press F12 to render.

6) Right now, the text is flat. Now to make it 3D, go to the Editng Buttons (F9). In the Curves and Surfaces panel, there are two settings that can make the text look 3D quickly. The first one is to click on Extrude 3 times, to give the text a depth of .3 Blender Units. This gives the text thickness.

8) In the Curves and Surfaces panel, click on Bevel 2 times. Another thing we can do to make the text more striking is to bevel the edges. To do that, press the Bevel key twice to give the text a bevel depth of .02 Blender units. Press F12 to render.

9) We can also change the orientation of the text. In the Font panel, for example, we can center the text by clicking on Center. We can also change the font to any font that is installed on your PC. The default font is <builtin>. To change it, on my Windows machine, from the Font panel, click the Load button. Navigate to the Windows/Fonts directory. The fonts that Blender supports are

highlighted with a dark blue square. I changed the font to Georgia Bold. To add a dramatic effect, I changed the spacing to 1.3 from the default of 1.

10) We can change the color of the text. Let's make it blue. Press F5 to go to the Shading buttons. Click the little icon to the left of Add New. Let's use the default Material, which comes with Blender's default scene, associated with the cube. It is still available, although the O in front of it shows that no object is associated with it. Click on Material. Change the color to Blue (R=0, G=0, B=1). Press the G key to grab the text and center it in the camera view. Press F12 to render.

8) So far, the blue text is offset against a blue sky. Let's get rid of the sky, to make the blue text stand out against a black background. Go to the Scene buttons (F10). We could, of course, make the World background color black. Another way is, from the Render Layers tab, we can get rid of the sky by clicking on the Sky button so that the sky doesn't render. Press F12 to render. Now the text is in the foreground, with a black background.

9) To get an even more dramatic effect for our text, we can add Ambient Occlusion. AO is a way of highlighting dark and light areas in the text. To do this, press F5 for the Shading buttons. Then go to the World buttons. Select AmbOcc. Click on Ambient Occlusion. We want to use Approximate AO, and both lighten and darken. So click on Approximate, and Both. Press F12 to render. Note both the darkening and lightening of the text.

10) Let's animate the text. To do this, go to Frame 1. With the cursor in the 3D window, press the I key to insert a keyframe. Select LocRot for location and rotation.

11) Go to Frame 230 Rotate the text 90 degrees along the Y axis (R Y 90. Press the I key to insert a keyframe. Select LocRot.

12) With the cursor in the 3D window, press ALT+A to animate.

13) To create an animation, go to the Output tab in the Scene buttons. If you enter // in Windows, you set the output animation to the same place where the blend file is. You can set the output to AVI (raw, Codec, or JPeg), QuickTime (for a MOV file), or FFMpeg.

There you have it. Animated 3D text in Blender. I hope this gives you a good start toward making your own cool animated 3D text effects.

Bouncing Ball (2.49)

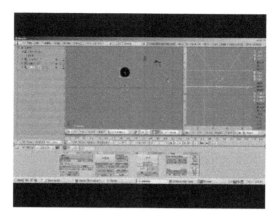

Watch the Video at: http://www.youtube.com/watch?v=BEY_6dFdUJY

At first glance, one might think that animating a bouncing ball would be easy, a simple matter of moving a sphere and adding location keyframes. Sure, the ball would move. However, it would not bounce realistically. Because of gravity, the ball moves slower at the top than at the bottom. The ball actually is stretched a bit in the middle of the bounce and squashes when it hits the floor. Because of friction, the height of the next bounce is less than the height of the previous bounce. The spin of the ball must be realistic as well.

We're not going to address all these things. The purpose of this tutorial, which is based on the Blender 3D Noob To Pro bouncing ball tutorial at http://en.wikibooks.org/wiki/Blender_3D:_Noob_to_Pro/Basic_Animation/Bounce, is to show the basics of animating a bouncing ball, including squashing the ball using lattice deformation and how to use IPO curves to bounce the ball a number of times without redoing the first bounce sequence again and again. I used Blender 2.49B.

We'll start by deleting the default cube (Right click, pressing the X key, and confirming the delete). Then add a UV Sphere (Space-Add-Mesh-UVSphere), accepting the default settings of 32 rings and 32 segments. From the editing buttons (F9), press Set Smooth. Then add a subsurf modifier at level 2. This gives us a nice round ball.

Press NUM1 to go into Front View. Add a Lattice (Space-Add-Lattice). Press Z to go into wireframe mode. Select the lattice. Scale the lattice so that the UV Sphere is inside of it, with the sides of the lattice touching the sides of the sphere.

To make the lattice control the sphere, select the sphere, then Shift Select the lattice. Press CTRL+P and choose the Lattice Deform option to make the lattice the parent of the sphere. Select the UV Sphere and press F9. Look at the modifier stack. You should see the phrase "Lattice parent deform" at the top of the stack. This means that the lattice modifier was applied correctly. To test this, select the lattice and scale or move it. The sphere mesh should scale or move as well. We'll use the lattice later to squash the ball. The Make Real button would make the lattice permanently control the ball. We can ignore this button for this simple tutorial.

Now it's time to animate the ball. To do this, switch to Scene SR:1-Animation. This built in scene setup has all the windows we need for animation - the Outline Window, the 3D viewport of course, the IPO window, which we'll use later, and the buttons window.

Position the 3D cursor in the 3D viewport and press NUM1 to go to Front View. The blue Z arrow should point upwards. We're going to animate the first bounce over 23 frames, which is about 1 second assuming a standard movie speed of 24 frames per second. Press F10 to go to the Scene buttons, and set the end frame to 23.

It's time to insert key frames. Note that we are animating the lattice, not the ball.

Make sure we're in Frame 1. If not, press SHIFT+Left Arrow or enter the number 1 in the Frame Number area. We start the animation when the ball is at the top of its bounce. Press the G key, then the Z key, to move the lattice up in the Z direction, about 7 Blender units or so, to the top of the bounce.

Press the I key and set a key for LocRotScale. Note how there are now 9 curves in the IPO window, for location, rotation, and scale, in the X, Y, and Z direction. You get 3 curves for each, for X, Y, and Z.

Go to Frame 11. Press the G key, then the Z key. Move the lattice down in the Z direction, to 1 Blender unit above the ground. This is where the ball will be squashed a bit. Press the I key and insert a LocRotScale key.

Go to Frame 13. Leave the Lattice in the same position and insert another LocRotScale key.

Go to Frame 23. Move the Lattice back to its position at Frame 1 by pressing the G key, then the Z key, then moving it back to 7 Blender Units up. In real life, the ball should move back somewhat less than that, because of friction, but for this tutorial, where the ball will just bounce forever, we can ignore this. Press I and insert a LocRotScale key.

We have animated the basic bounce. On Frame 12, we will squash the ball. Go to Frame 12. Place te cursor at the base of the lattice. Set the Pivot point to 3d Cursor. Scale the ball on the Z axis by pressing the S key and then the Z key. Press I to insert a LocRotScale key.

In IPO window, move the Green vertical bar back and forth to scrub the animation. We have now animated both the bounce and the squash. Pressing Alt A will also do the animation of the bounce forever. Press ESC to stop the animation.

The reason the ball bounces forever is that the animation is 23 frames long, exactly as long as the ball bounce. That's a coincidence. To demonstrate this, change the animation length to 250 frames. and press Alt A. Now the ball bounces and just stays there from frame 24 to 250 instead of bouncing. Suppose we want the ball to bounce forever no matter how long the animation. To do that, go to the IPO window. Press A to select all the curves. From the Curve Menu, select Extend Mode and select Cyclic. When you replay the animation, ALT+A, the ball bounces for the entire animation.

There's plenty more tweaking that can be done to this basic animation. You can add materials and textures to the ball. You can play with the IPO curves to control how the ball moves, stretches, and contracts. I hope this gets you started. Happy Blendering.

Blender 2.5 Animation, Part 1 (2.5)

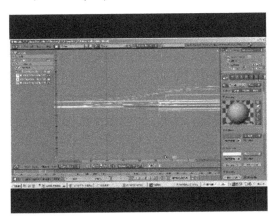

Watch the Video at: http://www.youtube.com/watch?v=0HA_FQVqaC4

This tutorial is based on the Blender 2.5 Tour 9 (Animation) video, published by Michael Fox, aka mfoxdogg. Michael works closely with the Blender developers and has detailed knowledge of all the new features in 2.5. At my blog, at http://blender3dvideos.blogspot.com, is a link to his animation tutorial, as well as to his blog at blenderlabrat.blogspot.com. He has been doing Blender 2.5 tours for a while now, as evidenced by the fact that this is Tour 9. What's nice is that Michael also frequently contributes comments to my videos as well. If you have 2.5 questions, just email him or post a response to his comment.

I won't go into nearly as much detail as Michael does. My goal for this video is to give you a basic understanding of how animation in 2.5 works, and how it differs from 2.4x animation. For one thing, animation is much easier in 2.5. For another, you can animate just about anything in 2.5. In 2.4x there were many features that you could not animate. The developers completely rewrote, and significantly improved, the animation code in 2.5.

So start up Blender 2.5. I'm using the Alpha 0 version, which you can download from blender.org. We'll start with the default cube. Just as in 2.4x, with the cursor in the 3D window, you can press the I key to insert a keyframe. You can insert combinations of location, rotation, and scale keyframes. At Frame 1, insert a LocRotScale to insert location, rotation, and scale keyframes. The timeline window is right below the 3D window.

Move the timeline slider to Frame 50. Move the cube 3 or 4 Blender
units to the right (Right click to select, G to grab, then drag, then
press ENTER). Scale the cube up 3 times (S - 3 - Enter). Rotate the
cube 45 degrees (R - 45 - Enter). Insert a LocRotScale keyframe
(press the I key, then select LocRotScale). Set the animation end
frame to 50 by entering 50 in the End area. Press ALT+A to animate.
Note how the cube grows, moves, and rotates from Frame 1 to Frame 50.
Press ESC to stop the animation.

SHIFT+ALT+A behaves a bit differently from Blender 2.4x. If you
press SHIFT+ALT+A, the animation goes backwards, from Frame 50 back
to Frame 1. You can see the backwards animation in the timeline, as
the slider goes backwards. In 2.4x SHIFT+ALT+A pleys the animation
forward in all windows. In the VCR controls in the timeline, you see
two arrows, a left pointing arrow and a right pointing arrow. The
left pointing arrow plays the animation backwards, and the right
pointing arrow plays the animation forwards.

Just as in 2.4x, you can animate material properties, such as diffuse
color. In 2.4x, you had to go to the material context and press I to
insert a keyframe. In 2.50, the material properties are grouped
together in the materials panel. Let's change the diffuse color from
red at frame 1 to green at frame 25 and blue at frame 40. First, go
to the materials panel by clicking on the grey ball icon. Then go to
Frame 1 by setting the current frame number. A basic goal of Blender
2.5 is that anything that you see can be keyframed. The way to do
that is to right click on a property and then select Insert Keyframe.
Click on the Diffuse Color rectangle. Change it to a reddish color
by selecting it in the color wheel. Right click on the rectangle and
choose Insert Keyframes. Keyframes are inserted for the Red, Green,
Blue, and Alpha channels.

Now go to Frame 25 by setting the Current Frame slider. Click on the
Diffuse Color rectangle. Change the color to a greenish color.
Right click on the diffuse color rectangle. Select Insert Keyframes.

Go to Frame 40 by setting the Current Frame slider. Click on te
Diffuse Color rectangle. Change the color to something blue like.
Right click on the diffuse color rectangle. Select Insert Keyframes.
Now press ALT+A. Now the cube grows, moves, rotates, and changes
color, based on the keyframes you have set.

You can add bunch of properties at a time, including properties you
could not set in 2.4x. You do this by defining a keying set. Here's
how it's done. We're going to change a group of properties related
to specularity, the little spot that's reflected from the lamp. To
do this, go to Frame 1, in the usual way. Right click on the
Specular color rectangle. Click on Add Single To Keying Set. Then

right click on the Specular Shader. Click Add Single to Keying Set. Right click on Hardness. Click Add Single to Keying Set. We've now defined properties related to specularity that we can keyframe all at once. At Frame 1, change Specular color to magenta, Shader to Phong, and Hardness to 255.

Click the little Key icon next to the word ButtonKeyingSet. This keyframes all those specular properties. Go to Frame 33. Change Specular color to yellow, Shader to Blinn, and Hardness to 3. Click the Key Icon next to the word ButtonKeyingSet. Keyframes are added at that point. If you press ALT+A, you might not see all the changes, but if you created an actual video, you would see it.

At this point, if you have worked in 2.4x with animation, you might be wondering where all these curves are kept and whether you can edit them in the IPO window. Well, I have news for you. The IPO Curve Editor is gone. Now you're probably even more confused. The IPO Curve Editor has been replaced by the Graph Editor. These curves are, after all, graphs. The graphs are grouped in a way that you really can edit them easily. The curves are grouped into action oriented curves (the location, rotation, and scale curves), and the Materials oriented curves. The Button Keying Set, when expanded, shows the curves related to specularity, that we defined in the keying set. If you collapse the Button Keying Set, you see the diffuse color curves.

How can you edit just one curve? By clicking on the eye icon, you can hide (or show) a particular curve. You can hide or show all the curves in a keying set by clicking on its eye icon. If you click enough eyes, you can get down to the particular curve you want to edit. By the way, these curves are now called F-curves. These curves are Bezier curves, just as in 2.4x. I'll discuss the Graph Editor, as well as the other visual editors related to animation, in Part 2 of the 2.5 Animation Tutorial.

I hope this gives you a leg up on how animation has changed in Blender 2.5. If you want to play with the Blend file I created, go to my blog related to this tutorial, at blender3dvideos.blogspot.com.

Blender 2.5 Animation, Part 2 (2.5)

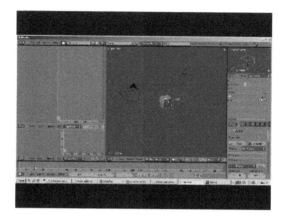

Watch the Video at: http://www.youtube.com/watch?v=3VCJ6hFDXCE

In my first animation video, I showed how to keyframe location, rotation, scale, and material color, as well as how to group keyframed properties into keying sets. I left you probably wondering how, considering that the IPO window has disappeared, you can change the curves by editing them as you could do in Version 2.4x. In this video, I will show you how this is done, and how, overall, the animation process is easier than before. We will also look at some properties that now can be keyframed, such as modifiers, as well as the new F-Curve system.

Here's the recipe:

1) Start with the default scene, with the default cube. Change to the Animation view. In the Animation view, there are a number of new windows, in addition to the 3D window. The three that specifically relate to animation are on the left part of the screen. At the top is the Dopsheet, which is the new name for the Action Editor. As before, pressing CTRL+down arrow makes the window full screen. We'll be doing this a lot in this video, to see what's going on in a particular window. Pressing CTRL+down arrow again returns the window to its original size.

In the middle left part is the Graph Editor, which is the new version of the 2.4x IPO Editor. You can edit animation curves in the Graph Editor. The organization of the curves has been redone, with major enhancements which I'll point out as we go.

At the bottom right corner is the timeline, the window which has changed the least. As before, you can scrub the animation by dragging the vertical green arrow, and the VCR llke keys do roughly what they did before. As I mentioned in the 2.50 Animation Part 1 tutorial, you can now run the animation backwards.

Before we start, set the end frame of the animation to 50 frames by entering 50 in the End area of the Timeline.

We're going to insert a LocRotScale keyframe at Frame 1, to start the animation process. It works the same way. Position the cursor over the 3D window. Press the I key. Select LocRotScale. Let's see what happened. It looks like there were some curves added in the Graph Editor. Press CTRL+Down Arrow to see what was added. We can't see what curves were added until we click on the left arrow, to expand the display.

Nine curves indeed were added, location, rotation, and scale, in the X, Y, and Z direction, as in 2.4x. The rotation curve has a new term - Euler - that wasn't there before. That's because rotation can be done in what's called Quaternions, as well as Eulers. For the time being, ignore this. Eulers are what we know as XYZ. We'll go into more detail about these curves after we actually animate the cube.

Press CTRL+Down Arrow to return the Graph Editor back to its original size.

Go to Frame 25. Press the G key and drag to move the cube over 4 or 5 Blender Units. Press Enter when done. Scale the cube up 2 times (S - 2 - Enter). Rotate the cube 45 degrees (R - 45 - Enter). Press the I key and insert an LoRotScale keyframe. Let's see what happened in the various graphs.

Start with the Graph Editor. Indeed, there are now 9 curves that we can see. They're all visible because all the check boxes at the left are checked. There's also an individual color assigned to each curve, such as red for the cube's X location. Let's in fact edit the curve for the cube's X location. To do that, uncheck all the boxes except for the X location curve. As before, each curve (they're now called F-curves) is a Bezier curve. You're in edit mode, with all the points, each representing a keyframe, selected. Press A to deselect all. Then right click on the ending keyframe. Move it up 2 Blender units or so by pressing the G key and moving it up. If you uncheck the Cube group and then check it again, all the curves display.

The lock icon controls whether or not a particular curve can be edited. If you click on it, the lock icon goes into the locked position and it can't be edited. If you click on it again, the curve is unlocked and can be edited.

Press CTRL+Down Arrow to return the Graph Editor to its original location.

Press ALT+A to run the animation. The cube goes in the X direction, according to how you edited it.

The eye icon controls whether or not that particular curve contributes to the animation. It's a toggle. When the curve contributes to the animation, you see an eye. When it doesn't, the icon is greyed out. To show you how it works, click on all the eyes except the one associated with the X location curve. Press CTRL+Down Arrow to return the Graph Editor back to its original location. Press ALT+A or use the VCR keys to animate. Now the cube just moves in the X direction.

While we were animating, note that the Dopesheet, the graph at the top right part of the screen, was populated. Position the cursor over the Dopesheet and press CTRL+Down Arrow. These are actions that can be combined in the NLA editor. We won't discuss these in this video. I just wanted to point this out. There still seem to be some problems with screen refreshing of this window.

Let's see what happens when we animate another object. Let's add Suzanne to the scene (SHIFT+A, Add, Mesh, Monkey). Let's insert a LocRotScale keyframe for her. Press the I key, then select LocRotScale. Some more curves were added. Amazingly, we can edit the curves of both objects. What happened? First, Suzanne is now called "Mesh". There's an object called Mesh, as well as a mesh called "Mesh". As with the cube, the curves for what we used to know as Suzanne are in the Mesh's mesh. If you expand the Mesh Mesh, you'll see them. You can also view the Cube's curves.

Press ALT+Down Arrow to return the Graph Editor back to its original position.

The last thing I'll show in this video is that modifiers can be keyframed. This can make for amazing effects. Let's add an Array Modifier to the monkey. Set the current frame to 1. Then, click on the Modifier icon in the Mesh's Properties. Select Array. Change the count to 4. With the cursor on Count, in the Array Modifier area, right click. Select Insert Keyframe. Then go to Frame 25.

Change the count to 2. With the cursor on Count, select Insert Keyframe. Press ALT+A to run the animation. Note how the number of monkeys changed.

Look at the Graph Editor. A new curve, called Count(Array) was created. There also is a Count(Array) curve created in the Dopesheet.

The goal is that any property you can see can be animated. Think of all the modifiers and all their properties that you can now animate easily.

Believe it or not, this only scratches the surface. I hope this tutorial gets you to think about how to use Blender 2.5's animation in your scenes.

Armature Animation (2.49)

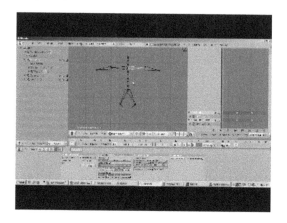

Watch the Video at: http://www.youtube.com/watch?v=19JqKOOG1IY

The purpose of this video is to show how armature animation works in Blender 2.49b. Understanding how to move the bones in an armature is the key to being able to rig a character. We'll first create a basic skeleton-like armature. Then, I will show the difference between FK (Forward Kinematics) and IK (Inverse Kinematics). I like IK in particular because my initials are IK. It's also something we both have in common with the exquisitely unreadable German philosopher, Immanuel Kant.

Leaving the Categorical Imperative aside, we will create a simple hand wave cycle and introduce the Action Editor and the Non Linear Action Editor (NLA Editor), to give you an idea of how actions are defined and how they can be layered together to produce complex movement. We're concentrating on the armature only, how the skeleton moves, so to speak, not the object to be rigged. Once you have an armature, say, of a human, moving correctly, you can then rig it to a human-like object. This is the theory behind the ManCandy rig. I will discuss skinning, the process of associating an armature with a character, either 2 or 4 footed, or I guess any-other-number-of-footed creature, in another tutorial.

Steps:

1) Delete the default cube. We're going to create a primitive skeleton. Go to Animation view by selecting it from the View dropdown. Go to Front View (NUM1). Add an armature (Space - Add - Armature). Scale the bone up 4 times (S - 4 - Enter). Look at the

Outliner. Expand the Armature outline. Note that the Armature has
one bone, called Bone.

Tab into Edit mode. A bone is a child object to the armature. A
bone has three parts, the tip, the root, and the body. A bone can be
selected in one of two ways. One way is to select the bone's body,
which will also select the bone's tip and root. The other way is to
right click on the body and shift right click on the root, which
selects the body, which is between the tip and the root. Press W for
the Specials menu. Select Subdivide Multi, with 4 cuts. So now we
have 5 bones, which can function as a primitive spinal cord.
Expanding the Armature display in the outliner shows that the bones
are named Bone.001, Bone.002, Bone.003, and Bone.004, parented to
Bone. You can also see the names in the 3D view by going to the Edit
buttons (F9) and pressing the Names button. Press the Names button
again to turn the names off.

2) Turn on X-Axis Mirror. This is a handy tool which lets you
create mirrored bones on the X axis. When the bones are symmetrical,
using X axis mirror means that you only need to create bones on one
side. Mirrored bones are created on the other side. Normally, to
simply add a bone, you press the E key, which extrudes the bone.
However, with X-axis mirror turned on, you can add mirrored bones by
pressing SHIFT+E. If X-Axis Mirror is turned off, SHIFT+E acts like
the E key, just extruding one bone. we'll also mirror extrude 2 legs
with SHIFT+E.

Here's how it works. We're going to create two primitive arm bones,
on the left and the right, at the same time. With the tip of the 4th
bone of the "spine" selected, press SHIFT+E. This creates two bones,
on the left and the right, which can be scaled. Press Enter when the
bones are at the desired size. Select the tip of the newly created
bone on the right and press SHIFT+E again. This creates two more
mirrored bones.

We can create mirrored legs. Select the root of the lowest bone of
the armature. Press SHIFT+E to create two "legs". Then select the
tip of the bone on the lower right. Press SHIFT+E to create two more
bones, for the feet. I hope you get the idea. I'll leave it to you
to create fingers and hands, but for now, we have the basic skeletal
bone strucure.

Let's see how bones are named. From the Editing buttons, in the
Armature panel, click on Names. Names shows you the names of the
bones that were generated. An easy way to see how the bones are
named is by using the Outliner. The original bone is called Bone.
The spine bones were created with the suffix .001, .002, .003, when
the big bone was subdivided. Mirrored bones, the ones created with

SHIFT+E, have an additional _R and _L, depending on whether they are
created on the left or the right. Look at the outliner. You can see
that each leg is parented off the base bone, Bone. If you look at a
detailed armature, such as the Mancandy rig, you'll see that the
bones have meaningful names, like Left Arm, Right Pinky, and so on.

The outliner clearly shows parent-child relationships in the
armature. This is important when we start posing the armature. Turn
off names.

3) OK. Now we have a basic skeleton. Let's see how the bones move,
in particular the difference between forward kinematics (FK) and
Inverse Kinematics (IK). Blender has a special mode, called Pose
Mode, allowing us to move bones so that the armature ends up in the
position we want. We're going to create a simple arm wave, what
Blender calls an Action. Blender has a special mode, called Pose
Mode, for moving armature bones. We're at Frame 1. Select the two
bones for the right arm (Right click on the arm, then SHIFT+Right
click on the second bone). Press the I key. Select LocRot.

The curves don't appear in the IPO Curves editor, although they were
created. The reason you don't see the curves is that you need to go
to the Pose curves. Change the curve type from Object to Pose.

A handy feature in the timeline is the red button that automatically
records keyframes as you move bones around. If you don't press it,
you would need to remember which bones you moved as you keyframe.
This way, Blender keyframes each move as you do it.

Now go to Frame 11 by pressing Up arrow or entering the number 11 in
the current frame area. Select the arm bone and press the G key to
move it up a bit. Then select the other arm bone and press the G key
to move it up in a salute type position.

We've actually created half of the waving action. We'll complete it
now. Switch the window from the IPO editor to the Action Editor.
Note that there are 2 keyframed bones, Bone.003_L, and
Bone.003_L.001. The diamonds indicate the keyframe. To complete the
wave, select the two diamonds (they're yellow when selected and white
when unselected), at Frame 1. Then press SHIFT+D to copy. Finally,
drag the two diamonds to Frame 21. Drag the vertical green arrow and
watch the wave. Press CTRL+DownArrow to maximize the Action Editor.
Rename the action to Wave, from Action. Press CTRL+DownArrow to
return the Action Editor to it's original position.

Let's see the difference between FK and IK. Select the right arm
bone. Turn on the AutoIK button. Grab the arm and move it. Note
how the whole skeleton, except for the legs, move. This is
definitely not how an arm moves. It's actually more appropriate for
a leg. IK actually does movement backwards, to the root of the
skeleton. You can change how far back the IK calculates by
disconnecting a bone. To show this, select the third bone, go into
Edit Mode (Tab), and click the CON button, which disconnects this
bone. Go back into Pose Mode. Select the arm again, and move it.
Note that the movement stops at the disconnected bone. FK does
movement forwards.

There's one last window to see, the NLA Editor. This lets us mix
different types of actions. Change the window type to NLA Editor.
You should see the Wave action. If you press the C key while the Wave
action is highlighted, you're prompted to change the action to an NLA
Strip. Press Enter. These strips can be combined (wave + walk + hip
swivel + talk, and so on). A detailed explanation of the NLA Editor
is the subject of a future tutorial.

So that's a brief look into the basics of animating an armature. I
hope you enjoyed it.

IPO Drivers and PyDrivers (2.49)

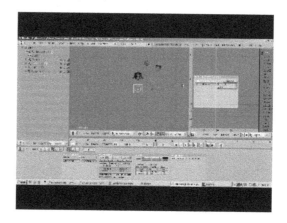

Watch the Video at: http://www.youtube.com/watch?v=2JaSguOBHbw

With basic Blender animation, you create keyframes at different
frames in your animation, and then Blender's IPO system fills in the
blanks (the technical term is "interpolates") values for the frames
in between. Sometimes you might want to base a particular part of
the animation of one object, such as its location, rotation, or size,
on the action of another object. This is where IPO drivers come into
play. For even more sophisticated control, you can create a Python
expression to do some really wild things. The purpose of this video
is to introduce you to both IPO drivers and Python drivers (aka
PyDrivers) so that you can really spice up your animations.

Here's the recipe:

1) Keep the default cube.   Add Suzanne above the cube. Get rid of
the 3D Transform widget, which gets in the way of this demonstration.

2) Go to the setup menu. Choose SR1-Animation. The animation setup
is very convenient for animation. It consists of an outline window
on the extreme left, a 3D window on the middle, and an IPO Curve
Editor window on the right. Additionally, there is a timeline window
under the 3D window and IPO Curve Editor window, and a Buttons window
at the bottom.

3) Let's animate the monkey's movement along the X axis. We'll set
the length of the animation to 50 frames by setting the End frame to
50. We're at Frame 1. Insert a Loc keyframe by pressing the I key
and selecting Loc. Move to Frame 50. Note how the vertical green
line in the IPO window moves to Frame 50 as well. Move the monkey 5

Blender units to the right. Then press the I key and select Loc.
Note that a curve is generated in the IPO window. We can't see all
of it. To see all of it, from the View Menu of the IPO Curve Editor,
select All. Alternatively, you could have pressed the Home key.

Interestingly, there are 3 curves that were created, corresponding to
LocX, LocY, and LocZ. Left click on LocX. The highlighted curve a
curvy line, from 0 to about 5, corresponding to the Blender units on
the X axis for the monkey's position. There are 2 dots that
represent the end points of the curve, at frames 1 and 50. You
placed the monkey at a specific X location on Frame 1 and Frame 50.
Blender interpolates, in what's called a Bezier interpolation, the
monkey's location for the frames in between. The monkey speeds up in
the earlier frames, goes relatively constant, until the last 10 or so
frames, where the monkey slows down.

An alternative interpolation method is called Linear. In this case,
the monkey's speed is constant. Actually, Bezier is a more realistic
type of interpolation. Feel free to experiment. To change to
linear, select Curve - Interpolation Mode - Linear, from the IPO
Editor Window. Press SHIFT+ALT+A to animate, which animates no
matter where the cursor happens to be. Now the speed of the monkey is
constant. Press ESC to end the animation.

LMB on LocY. The monkey's Y location stays at roughly 3 Blender
units for the entire animation. Let's change that in the IPO Curves
Editor window. To do that, select LocY. Press Tab to go to Edit
mode. We're going to change the end Y location of the monkey. Right
click to select the end point. Press the G key. Left click and drag
to about 5 Blender units, giving a Bezier type curve in the Y
direction. Press ALT+Shfit-A to animate. Now the monkey goes up in
the Y direction as well as across in the X direction. Press ESC to
end the animation.

The LocZ curve also was created. The Z position of the monkey stays
at 0 no matter where we are. You won't see the Z location change in
top view because we're looking down, in the negative Z direction.
Press Num 1 to go to Front View. This time, we'll make the monkey
jump up and down. Press Tab to go to Edit mode. We'll change the
LocZ by adding a point on the curve. To do this, position the cursor
about halfway between the beginning and the end and press CTRL+LMB.
This creates a new point. Press the G key and drag the curve up 3
Blender units. Press SHIFT+ALT+A to animate. The monkey jumps up
and down. Press ESC to end the animation.

4) Great! We've animated the monkey in 3 directions. Now suppose
we want to make another object, like the cube, follow the monkey. If
you SHIFT+LMB on LocX, LocY, and LocZ, you'll see that our animation

is a bit complicated to copy. Select the cube. Trying to copy these curves is tedious. Also, if we change the monkey's animation, we'd have to redo the cube's animation. Very quickly, I think we'd give up.

This is where IPO drivers come into play. We want the cube to follow the monkey in the X direction no matter where the monkey goes. To do that, select the LocX channel (that's the technical name) in the IPO Curves Editor. We're going to add a driver. Click the Add Driver button. In the Ob: area, enter the name of the monkey mesh, Suzanne. There are 9 possible channels that can drive the cube. Select LocX. Note the dotted rectangle icon representing a driven LocX channel. Press SHIFT+ALT+A to animate. See how the cube follows the monkey across.

5) With a PyDriver, we can get even more cute. Suppose we want the cube to follow only at half the speed of the monkey in the X direction. Press the N key in the IPO Curves window to bring up the Transform Properties window. Press the little snake icon (I guess it's a python). You can enter a Python expression, in this case:

ob("Suzanne").LocX/2

Make sure you enter this exactly, observing the case. Otherwise, Python will give you an error message. Press SHIFT+ALT+A to animate. Note that the cube is only going half as fast as Suzanne in the X direction. Press NUM7 to go to Top View. Press SHIFT+ALT+A to animate. The animation works the same way in top view. This would not work be possible with a simple IPO driver. You can animate multiple objects. Try doing a "monkey race" with different denominators for each monkey's speed relative to other monkeys. You can also animate rotation and scale. Imagine the possibilities. This animation can be used in the game engine, as your aliens and monsters fight each other.

Nodes

Composite Nodes (2.49)

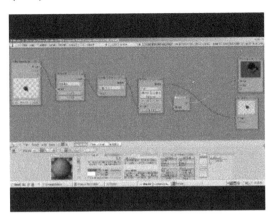

Watch the Video at: http://www.youtube.com/watch?v=AAnxoJsdAAM

Nodes are a powerful Blender feature, allowing you to change how your scene renders, to combine images and videos, and to do many types of special effects. Compositing is a critical part of the video production process. The purpose of this video is to make you comfortable moving around in the Node Editor and to introduce a some basic image effects.

Let's delete the default cube and have fun with Suzanne. So highlight the cube (right click), press X to delete and Enter to confirm. Then add Suzanne (space-add-mesh-monkey). Press F9 to go to the Edit buttons. Press the Set Smooth button to make her look a bit more presentable. Add a red material by pressing F5 (Shading), then the Add New button to add a new material. Set the R to 1, the G to 0, and the B to 0.

To set up node based rendering, press F10 to go to the Scene buttons. In the Anim panel, press the Do Composite button. When you do this, instead of the scene rendering, the result of your composite node processing renders when you press F12.

To go to the Node Editor, change the View type to Node Editor. Blender supports material nodes and texture nodes as well as composite nodes. To enable Composite Nodes, click the Face icon. Then, click on the Use Nodes button.

Two puzzling rectangular objects display. On the left is the Render Layers node. On the right is the Composite node. You can resize a node by clicking on the lower right part of the node and dragging. The nodes are connected by a black wire, from the yellow Image button on the right side of the Render Layer node to the yellow Image button on the left side of the Composite node. What's going on?

Composite nodes really have three types, Input, Output, and different types of things you might do to the input before you render the output. Think of compositing as similar to going to the barber shop. Your head, before you get your haircut, with unshaven and with unkempt hair, is the input. The barber can do a number of things – give you a shave, wash your hair, cut it short, and so on. These are like processing nodes. The end result – the output – ends up in the Composite Node. The first big rule of compositing is: There Can Only Be One Composite Node.

The Render Layers node is the input – your scene before anything is done with it. The Composite node is the result. Node setups can get very confusing. The easiest way to set them up is to place the input nodes (there can be more than one, because we might combine things, such as a scene with an image), on the far left, and the output node, the Composite node, to the right. The processing nodes are in the middle, best placed in logical order from left to right.

Move the Composite node all the way to the right. Moving is similar to moving in the 3D window. Press the Right arrow key to select the Composite node, then drag it all the way to the right. The wire follows along.

Press F12 to render. Suzanne renders as if there was no compositing active. You also see a thumbnail of the rendered scene both in the Render Layers node and the Composite node. That's because this is like walking into the barber shop, seeing the long line, and walking out. Nothing was done.

OK. Let's do some stuff to Suzanne. How about making her 3 times bigger? Easy. Instead of going back to the 3D view and scaling her up, you can do it in the Node editor. Add a Scale Node (Space - Add - Distort - Scale). Nothing happens yet. You need to connect the wires. To do this, connect the Image socket (that's the yellow Image dot) on the right side of the Render Layers node to the Image socket on the left side of the Scale node. This tells the Node editor to pump the scene, with Suzanne, into the Scale node. Set the X and Y values to 3, to indicate how large to scale Suzanne.

Next, connect the Image socket on the right side of the Scale node to the Image socket on the left side of the Composite node. This tells the Node editor to take the new, larger Suzanne, and add it as input to the Composite node. Look at the image on the Composite node. It already shows the bigger Suzanne. If you press F12 to render, Suzanne also renders larger.

That's a good start. How about flipping her upside down? Easy. Add a Flip node (Space - Add - Distort - Flip). Connect the Image socket on the right side of the Scale node to the Image socket on the left side of the Flip node. From the dropdown, select Flip X & Y. Now connect the Image socket on the right side of the Flip node with the Image socket on the left side of the Composite node.

The path is clear. Suzanne is scaled and then flipped. You can see each step. By the way, the 3D view hasn't changed. Suzanne is still her old self. Change to 3D view, look, and change back to the Node editor.

The Viewer node, another type of output node, lets you view Suzanne's progress. To add a Viewer node, press Space - Add - Output - Viewer. Automatically, the Viewer node is connected, via the Image socket, to the last node selected. A handy button is the Use Backdrop button, which displays the most recently selected Viewer node. You see Suzanne both scaled and flipped.

We can see Suzanne after she was scaled but before she was flipped. To do that, cut the connection between the Flip node and the Viewer node by pressing the left mouse button and dragging across the wire. Then, connect the output Image socket of the Scale node to the input Image socket of the Viewer node. Now Suzanne is scaled but unflipped.

Click the Backdrop button to get the regular background. Let's blur Suzanne, giving the illusion of fuzziness. Blur is a filter node. So press Space - Add - Filter - Blur. Connect the Image socket on the right side of the Flip node to the Image socket on the left side of the Blur node. Set X and Y to 10, specifying the blur amounts. Then connect the Image socket on the right side of the Blur node with the Composite node's image socket. Click the Backdrop button.

Now let's make Suzanne black and white. Add a Converter node to do that (Space - Add - Converter - RGB to BW). Convert the Image socket on the right of the Blur node to the Composite Node image socket.

Many of the keys you are familiar with in navigating the 3D window work in the node editor. Right click selects a node. Shift Right click on another node extends it. X deletes the selected nodes. CTRL+Z corrects your error.

You can group nodes when you have a lot of them. Let's say you really like to scale, flip, blur, and make objects black and white. You can create a group out of these nodes. Select all of them press CTRL+G. You've created a nice node group, cleaning up the diagram a lot. Node groups can be copied and even exported to another blend file, which is nice because you won't have to redo all those steps each time. The tab key shows the nodes in the group. If you change your mind, ALT+G undoes the grouping.

To summarize, we've enlarged Suzanne 3 times, flipped her over, blurred her, and got rid of her red color - all without touching the underlying 3D view, which you can see in the Render Layers node. This just scratches the surface. I hope this gives you a good start on compositing nodes in Blender. Happy Blendering!

Mix Node (2.49)

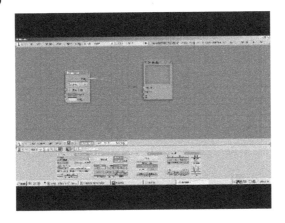

Watch the Video at: http://www.youtube.com/watch?v=AKH0LyZYQyQ

One of the powerful reasons for using Blender is that it can do just about all the steps in video production, from pre production right through post production, by itself. Although you might want to call on another product, such as an external renderer like Yafaray or an image editor such as the Gimp or Photoshop, for some specialized needs, in many cases Blender can do the job. The fewer pieces of software you have to juggle in your workflow, the better. Importing and exporting files between programs is a royal pain. Enhancing the quality of the color of images is one of these areas. When combined with Blender's composite node system, which I discussed in a basic way in a previous Youtube video, Blender can do just about everything a 2D image editor such as the Gimp or Photoshop can do.

In this tutorial, I will show how to use the Mix Node to blend two colors. This is a start to get you comfortable with tweaking 2D images entirely in Blender. This is just the tip of the iceberg. There is plenty of material, just in color processing, for many more tutorials. We'll spend the entire time in the Node Editor, pretending that Blender is really Photoshop in disguise. I will use Blender 2.49b.

Steps:
1) Start up Blender. One tiny bit of housekeeping before we go into the Node Editor. Press F10 to go to the Scene buttons. Press the Do Composite button in the Anim section, telling Blender's renderer to look at the composite nodes. Change the window type to Node Editor. That's where we'll stay. There are actually three types of node editing - Material, Composite, and Texture. We want the middle icon, the one with the face, the Composite Node. Click Use Nodes. Two

nodes display, the input Render Layer and the output Composite.
Delete the Render Layer node - we will ignore the 3D part of Blender.
To do that, select the Render Layer node (Right Click just like
you're selecting an object) and press the DEL key. We still need the
Composite Node, however, because that is what ultimately renders.
Move the Composite Node all the way to the right by selecting and
dragging it.

2) We're going to start by mixing two RGB colors. The Mix node is
the most important node in color editing. To add a Mix Node, press
SHIFT+A (the Space Bar also works), then Add - Color - Mix. Note
that there are 3 sockets on the left (the top one is grey and the
bottom 2 are yellow), for input into the node, and one on the right,
out from the Mix node after the node does its thing.

We'll concentrate on the bottom two yellow sockets. These are what
the Mix Node is going to mix. To the left of each socket is a grey
rectangle, along with the word Image. The grey rectangle represents
a color. The word Image means that an Image can be mixed. Actually,
you can mix one image with another, an image with a color, or one
color with another color. We'll start by mixing one color with
another. This is not really that common, but it works well for this
tutorial, to explain how the Mix Node works.

3) Click on the top rectangle. Make it red (R=1, G=0, B=0). Then
click on the bottom rectangle. Make it green (R=0, G=1, B=0).
Connect the output image socket of the Mix node with the input image
socket of the Composite Node. Press F12 to render. The result is a
big square which is a light green. What did the Mix Node do? We can
find out by positioning the cursor inside the render window, holding
down the left mouse button, and dragging. There's a text display of
the values of the particular pixel that the mouse is over. The
display shows the pixel X and Y coordinates, the RGB color values,
and the Alpha value. In this case, it doesn't matter because the
color is the same no matter where you click. The RGB color is
reported in two notations: R=128, G=128, and B=0, or R=.5, G=.5, and
B=0. One is the decimal representation, the other the Blender
representation of the color. What happened is that the Mix Node
mixed half of the red with half of the green.

This result is actually misleading, because one might think that this
"mix" is like mixing half of the red with half of the green as a
result of the Fac setting. Fac., which is set at .5, or 50%, stands
for Factor. But what is it actually factoring?

Let's find out. Set Factor to 1, or 100%. Press F12 to render. Now
the result is all green (R=0, G=1, B=0). There's no red in the
result at all.

Now set Factor to 0. Press F12 to render. Now the result is red, with no green at all.

What's happening is that for the Mix operation, the bottom color or image acts like the foreground, and the Factor is the percentage of the foreground's pixel values (each pixel being evaluated individually) that is used. Whatever percentage is not used is used by the top color. So, when Factor is 0, none of the green is used and all of the red. When Factor is .5 green and red are used equally, and when Factor is 1, all of the green is used and none of the red.

4) Now things get even more interesting. Click on the Mix dropdown list. Mix one of 16 possible ways that one image or color can be combined with another image or color. We can't possibly cover all of these in one 10 minute tutorial. But we can get a good start. Let's look at Add. Set the Factor to .5. Press F12 to render. Now we get an entirely different result: an orange square. What did Factor do this time? Clicking and dragging on the render square tells us that the result is R=1, G=.5, and B=0, all the red and 1/2 the green.

What did Factor do this time? Set Factor to 1 and press F12 to render. Now we get yellow (R=1, G=1, and B=0).

Set Factor to 0 and press F12 to render. Now we get Red (R=1, G=0, and B=0).

What happened? No matter what the factor, we always get all of the red. However, the amount of green is dependent on the Factor. On a pixel by pixel basis, the bottom color, multiplied by the factor, is added to the top color. Since the bottom color is green, the Factor controls, in effect, the amount of green in the result, with all of the red contributing.

5) Let's look at Subtract, which works a bit differently. With the Factor set to 0, press F12 to render. The result is red.

Set the Factor to .5. Press F12 to render. The result is still red.

Set the Factor to 1. Press F12 to render. The result is still red.

What's going on? If you look closely at the render text display, you'll see that while Red = 1, G actually equals -1. That's because

Subtract subtracted the green (1) from the Red's green value (0),
giving -1. Set Factor to .5. G now equals -.5 and R=1. That still
means a red result because any number less than zero means no green.

This is just the tip of the iceberg. Experiment with the other Mix
modes to get a full sense of the capabilities of this amazing tool.

Checkerboard With Texture Nodes (2.5)

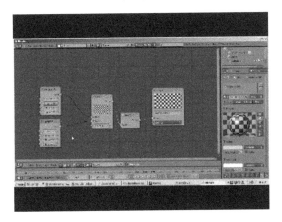

Watch the Video at: http://www.youtube.com/watch?v=9vE3k7dqDyc

The purpose of this video is both to introduce texture nodes in
Blender 2.5 and to familiarize you with the new Blender 2.5 user
interface. We are going to create a checkerboard, which you can
customize to any colors for the squares, without using any images.
We will create a checkerboard texture in the Node Editor, built from
Blender 2.5's built in checkerboard texture node. I used a mid-
September, 2009, pre-alpha build of Blender 2.5. When Blender 2.5 is
officially released, it's not guaranteed that the checkerboard
texture node, or any other node we will use, will still be there, but
it's quite likely. In fact, it's most probable that there will be
even more types of texture nodes available. By the way, this
tutorial should work in Blender 2.4x as well.

By creating your own textures in this way, you should have fewer
copyright problems than if you started with a JPEG image or some
other image you loaded from the Web. In addition, this method is
much more flexible. You can change the checkerboard colors any way
you like by just adjusting the color sliders.

We'll start by loading up Blender 2.5 and deleting the default cube.
Right click to highlight, then press the X key and confirm the
delete.

We'll work in Quad View. From the 3D View Menu, select Toggle Quad
View.

Add a plane (SHIFT+A - Add - Mesh - Plane).   Position the camera so
that it points directly down at the plane. Press ALT+R to clear
rotation. Then, from top view, move the camera so that it is
positioned at the center of the plane.

We're ready to create the checkerboard.   Highlight the plane, which
is where the checkerboard texture will be placed. Add a material to
the plane by clicking on the Material button in the bottom right
corner of the screen. Click on New. You don't need to set the color
or anything else for the material because, as you will see shortly,
the texture nodes control everything.

Switch to the Node Editor. There are a number of types of nodes you
can create in the Node Editor. The checkerboard icon is the one to
click for texture nodes. You can create all sorts of texture nodes
besides checkerboards. It just so happens that we're making a
checkerboard texture. Make sure that the Cube icon (Make Texture
Nodes From Object) is highlighted.   Click the New button to create a
new texture. Then check the Use Nodes check box.

The Node Editor has created two nodes for us.   On the left is a
Checkerboard node, with red and white squares.   Blender has a built
in checkerboard node, which you can access from Add Patterns Checker.
Its yellow color dot is connected to the yellow color dot on the
Output Node. Press F12 to render. The result is a red and white
checkerboard pattern. In Blender 2.5, texture nodes are used if they
are defined, by default.

This is a good start, but we don't have the right number of squares,
which should be 8 x 8. We have a 4 x 4 checkerboard. The solution:
reduce the size to .25 and render. Now we have an 8 x 8 red and
white checkerboard.

Nice going, but we're not finished. We're going to hook up two
texture nodes to let us change the colors of the red and white
squares. Position the checkerboard and the output nodes to the
right, to make room for two additional nodes. Go to the Add menu of
the Nodes Editor, click Color, then Compose RGBA. Connect the yellow
Color dot of the Compose RGBA node to the yellow Color1 dot of the
Checkerboard node. On the output node, the red squares turn black.
That's because the Compose RGBA node is now controlling what were
formerly the red squares. The RGB color settings for the RGBA node
are set to all zeros, for black.

The connections show what is happening. The input color for the
Compose RGBA settings are fed to the Color1 setting for the
checkerboard. Note that there is no color picker for Color1 in the

Checkerboard node any more. The color settings for the the checkerboard are connected to the Color1 setting for the output node, which is the one that is rendered.

Add another Compose RGBA Node on the left, and connect it to Color2 of the checkerboard node. Now the output is completely black. This makes sense because, as we saw, the default Compose RGBA Node color is black, so all the squares are black.

Now it's time to set the colors to whatever you like. Let's make our checkerboard blue and yellow. Simple enough. Set the top color to blue and the bottom to yellow. Yellow is the equivalent of Red=1 and Green=1. Incidentally, you can control the alpha settings, for transparency, here as well. Press F12 to render.

Changing the colors as changing the RGB sliders. You can get additional effects by simply adding more nodes. To illustrate, go to the Add Menu of the Node Editor, and go to Add Color Invert. Connect the Checkerboard yellow Color dot to the Add Invert Node color dot on the left side. Then connect the Add Invert yellow Color dot to the Output Node color dot. The result: the checkerboard colors are inverted, as you can see in each node, which shows the result.

I hope this shows you the power of texture nodes. We've really only scratched the surface.

Vector Blur (2.49)

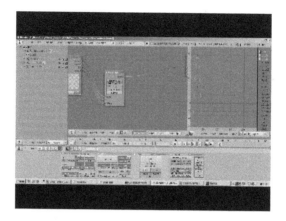

Watch the Video at: http://www.youtube.com/watch?v=qY4WcNqEXv8

Vector blur is a great way to add realism to your animation. Your eye naturally sees moving objects moving as a blur, because that is how your brain processes the motion. Without some sort of blurring, animated moving objects don't look as if they are realistically moving. Blender's animations are by default rendered as a sequence of perfectly still images. This is unrealistic, since fast moving objects do appear to be 'moving', that is, blurred by their own motion, both in a movie frame and in a photograph from a 'real world camera'.

To obtain such a blurring effect with moving objects, Blender can be made to render the current frame and some more frames, in between the real frames, and merge them all together to obtain an image where fast moving details are 'blurred'. The goal of this tutorial is to demonstrate how to blur moving objects in Blender.

First, we'll create a simple animation. We will animate the movement of the cube across the screen, over 50 frames. With an animation speed of 25 frames per second, that produces a 2 second video, one second going across the screen, the other second going back.

1) Go to the SR-1: Animation view.

2) Press the N key to bring up the Transform Properties window. Set the X location to -7, the Y location to 0, and the Z location to 0.

3) At Frame 1, press the I key and insert a Location key frame.

4) Go to Frame 25. Set the X location to 4, the Y location to 0, and the Z location to 0.

5) Press the I key and insert a Location key frame.

6) Go to Frame 50. Set the X location to -7, the Y location to 0, and the Z location to 0.

7) Press the I key and insert a Location key frame.

8) Go to the Scene buttons (F10), and set the animation to 50 frames.

9) In the Format panel, set the animation type to your favorite. I used the compressed AVI format with the CamStudio Lossless Codec, version 1.4, for compression.

The video will be created in the Output directory (/tmp by default), with a filename of 0001_0050.avi. Set the output directory to the folder where you want the video to be saved. If you chose a QuickTime movie, the filename would be 0001_0050.mov.

10) Hit the ANIM button. I will pause the video while the animation is being rendered, as I will do for the other animations in this video. The render took 1 minute, 10 seconds.

The animation does indeed have the cube move back and forth, but the motion of the cube is not realistic. The cube just moves in a straight line uniformly, without the blurring effect of motion.

With the help of the Node editor, we can introduce vector blur to this animation and compare. To do this,

1) Go to the Render Layers tab of the Scene button. Vector blur takes a special Vector (VEC) rendering pass, which is not rendered by default. Find the VEC button and enable it. Vector Blur requires the COMBINED, Z, and VEC passes. The others you may need to render the scene exactly as you need it.

2) Change the 3D view to the Node Editor. Press CTRL+Down Arrow to maximize te Node Editor. Click on the face, for composite nodes. Then click the USE NODES button. There are two default nodes, the input node (Render Layers) is the scene as rendered without compositing. The other node, the Composite node, is the final result of the compositing process.

3) Move the Composite Node all the way to the right, to make room for the Vector Blur.

4) Add the Vector Blur filter (Space - Add - Filter - Vector Blur). Accept the defaults. Connect the Image socket of the Render Layer to

the Image input of the Vector Blur node. Connect the Z socket of the
Render Layer node to the Z socket of the Vector Blur node. The Z
socket stores the Z information - the distance of the cube from the
camera. Connect the Speed socket of the Render Layer node to the
Speed socket of the Vector Blur node. The Speed socket is really the
key to blurring the cube's movement. You can play with the defaults.
Increasing the number of samples, for example, makes the vector blur
more realistic but slows down the rendering. Also, you can control
which moving objects are blurred. A speeding sports car should be
blurred, but bystanders should not.

5) Connect the Image output socket of the Vector Blur node with the
Image socket of the Composite node.

The noodle (the node setup) is complete. Go back to the Scene
buttons and click the Do Composite button. Press the Render button.
Look at Frame 1. The monkey is blurred.

6) Time to animate. Click the ANIM button. Pause until the 50
frames are rendered. The render took 1 minute, 47 seconds.

Now you see the cube blurred while it is moving --- a much more
realistic animation. Think of a fast sports car speeding by you.

Blender has another way to implement blurring a moving object: the
Motion Blur option. To demonstrate that, click the MBLUR button in
the Scene panel. Turn off Do Composite because motion blur doesn't
rely on nodes. MBLUR is very slow because it renders each frame up
to 16 times. The number of samples is controlled by the OSA setting,
which is 8 on my computer. Eight renders per frame is mighty slow.
The renderer calculates the position of each object and then averages
the positions out. It is more accurate than Vector Blur, but at the
cost of a LOT of time. Here is the cube animation with motion blur.

To summarize, Blender provides you with two options, Vector Blur and
Motion Blur, for making your moving object look more realistically
blurred as the object moves in the scene. For most applications,
especially in the Game Engine, Vector Blur will work well.

Physics and Particles

Fluid Simulation (2.49)

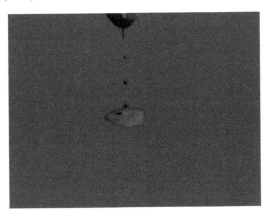

Watch the Video at: http://www.youtube.com/watch?v=wX5w1Kmsv_A

The purpose of this video is to show how the objects in Blender's fluid simulator work. We'll look at domains, obstacles, inflow, outflow, and of course fluid objects. Blender's fluid simulator at first seems very challenging. However, if you think about how fluids behave in real life - think of water pouring out of a faucet into a sink or a bathtub, the fluid simulator starts to become more logical. In this tutorial we're going to focus on the objects in Blender's fluid simulation.

Let's start with the most basic fluid simulation. At a minimum, the fluid simulator needs two things: a fluid, which can be free flowing like a waterfall or muddy like water in a pond; and a domain, which is an area in which the fluid lives. Be warned. This doesn't look exactly like water dripping from a faucet, but it does look like some icky gook falling down in a fluid like manner.

So start Blender. Usually we delete the default cube. This time, however, we will use the default cube. It will be the domain, the area in which the the fluid lives. Go to Front View, by pressing NUM1. The blue Z arrow will point up. We need this because fluids are affected by gravity. In Blender, Z is up and -Z is down.

Let's make the domain a bit higher along the z axis. Press the S key to scale, then the Z key, then scale the cube up 4 Blender units.

Grab it, with the G key, and move it along the Z direction (Z key) so
the domain sits on the X axis. Before we do anything with the cube,
duplicate it (SHIFT+D) and move it away from the original cube.
You'll see later why this is a good idea.

Just to track things, let's name our objects. Select the original
cube. Press the N key to bring up the Transform Properties window.
Rename the cube to Domain. Make sure the cube is in object mode.
Press Tab if the cube is in Edit mode.

To tell the fluid simulator that the cube is the domain, press the
Object buttons (F7), then the Physics button, the second button in
second group of buttons. Press the Fluid button the enable the fluid
simulator, on the extreme right. Click the Domain button.

Press the Z key to go into wireframe mode. You can see objects
inside of other objects in wireframe mode.

We need to add a fluid. Add an icosphere (Space - Add - Mesh -
Icosphere), accepting the default of 2 subdivisions. Scale it down
using the S key, so that the icosphere looks like a drop and is
positioned at the top part of the cube. Make sure that the icosphere
is inside the cube. Check out all the views and rotate, to make
sure.

In the Transform Properties window, rename the icosphere from Sphere
to Fluid. Let's make the fluid source green, just so we can see it.
Press F5 to add a material. To make the fluid source green, set R to
0, G to 1, and B to 0.

Select the domain and go to the material buttons. Make the domain
color red by setting R to 1, G to 0, and B to 0. Weird things happen
to the domain during the fluid simulation, as you'll see.

To tell fluid simulator that the icosphere is the fluid, make sure
the icosphere is in Object mode. Then press the Object buttons (F7)
and the Physics button. Press the Fluid button to enable the fluid
simulator. Click the Fluid button.

We're set up to run the fluid simulator. The cube is the domain and
the icosphere is the fluid. To run it, select the cube. In the
fluid simulator buttons for the cube, press the big BAKE button. The
cube turns into a blob and starts falling down like a drop. The
falling stops where the cube used to be, as if the cube was still
there, although it doesn't show.

Believe it or not, we've created a fluid animation. Press ALT+A to see it. Press ESC to stop the animation. The animation is done over 250 frames by default. To create an animation, press F10 (Scene buttons). Set the Output Directory to the directory where you want to store the animation. In the Output panel, navigate to the directory and then select Select Output Pictures. In the Format panel, select the type of video you want to create. The default is jpeg. I like the .avi format, with the CamStudio 1.4 Lossless Codec. I use CamStudio to capture screen shots for these tutorials. If you choose uncompressed the video will take a lot of space. Click the ANIM button and wait. The animation is being created, all 250 frames of it.

Depending on your computer, the animation can take a long time, up to 10 minutes.

Some things to note. The fluid looks too geometric to be believable. We can help this by smoothing the fluid. Select the domain object, which controls the color of the fluid as it falls. Go to the edit buttons. Press the Set Smooth button. Also, subsurfing the fluid will help. Add a subsurf modifier at Level 2. Select the domain. Press the BAKE button. For the sake of speed, let's reduce the number of frames to 50. At 25 frames per second, this is a 2 second video, but it illustrates the point.

Select the Fluid object. Go to the Physics buttons and change its type from Fluid to Inflow. Here's the result.

The fluid is more, well, fluid-like. An inflow is a fluid object that adds fluid. Blender allows more than one fluid source, i.e. more than one inflow, like more than one faucet or shower head. However, only one domain is allowed.

We're going to add an obstacle. Add a cube below the path of the fluid. Select the cube, making sure it's in Object Mode. Click on the Object buttons, then the Physics buttons. Go to the Fluid simulator. Enable Fluid and click on Obstacle. Running the fluid simulator produces the following result.

Finally, we're going to add an outflow, which takes fluid away from the simulator. An outflow is like a bathtub or faucet drain. To do this, add a plane above the cube, in the path of the fluid. Select the plane, in object mode. Go to the Fluid simulator, as before.

Enable Fluid and click the Outflow button. Select the domain and press the Bake button. The animation should look as shown, The fluid disappears before it hits the obstacle.

Remember the cube domain that we duplicated before? To make the simulation realistic, position it on the domain boundaries. You'll need to make it transparent and add materials and textures, no doubt. And probably you will want to apply a realistic water, oil, or mucky texture to your fluids. But that's it. We've done a basic fluid simulation, with a fluid and a domain. We've added an obstacle - in real life, something like a bathtub or sink, as well as an outflow, like a drain. I hope this gives you the basic idea of how it works.

Smoke Simulation (2.5)

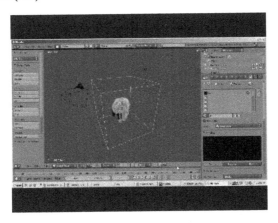

Watch the Video at: http://www.youtube.com/watch?v=y3C9FpCIBP4

Smoke simulation is a neat new feature of Blender 2.5. If you are familiar with Blender's particle system and the fluid simulation you should have no problem with blowing smoke in Blender 2.5. To make the smoke render, you need to create a volume type material and add a Voxel Data texture. These are new as well. I will demonstrate how to make smoke, from start to the the final animation and point out the new settings, which you can play with.

By the way, you can download the latest 2.50 Alpha version from blender.org. Since the developers are constantly making changes, make sure you have the latest and greatest.

So let's get started. Start with the default cube. Scale it 4 times (S - 4 - Enter). The large cube will be our domain, the area in which the smoke is generated. Press the Z key to go into wireframe mode, so we can see inside the cube. Then add a UV Sphere, within the domain (Shift-A, Mesh, UVSphere). The UVSphere will generate the smoke particles.

Select the cube. Select the Physics tab, all the way to the right. Scroll down until you see the Smoke section. Click the arrow. Click Add. Enable Smoke. Click Domain.

Select the UVSphere. Click Add. Click Flow. Next, go to the Particles tab, and click the Plus sign to add a Particle system. It is called ParticleSystem by default. Accept the default. Of course, you can tweak all the particle system settings later to make the smoke go wherever you want. Go back to the Physics tab, and the Smoke Section. Enter the ParticleSystem name under Particle System.

Press Alt-A to animate. We can see smoke coming out of the sphere.

We're not done yet. Press F12 to render. Only the cube renders. To get the smoke to render, you need to add a material and texture the cube domain in a new way.

Select the cube domain. Add a material. Click Volume. Play around with the transmission, scattering, emission color, transmission color, and reflection color. I set these to arbitrary values. I'm sure you can make much better smoke than I can.

Go to Texture button. Add a texture. Select Voxel Data. Make the domain Cube.

Press F12 to render. You can go on to animating by selecting the video type (MOV, AVI codec, AVI uncompressed), and set the number of frames. Then click the Animation button (Wow, they spelled out the word in full), and wait.

Here's the result from my random settings. I'm excited to see what kind of great smoke you can make. If you enjoyed this tutorial, don't forget to hit the big SUBSCRIBE button on Youtube. Happy Blendering.

Particles Basics (2.49)

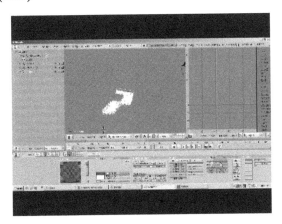

Watch the Video at: http://www.youtube.com/watch?v=dwsR8v5VE4M

Blender's particle system is flexible and powerful. It can be used
for simulating effects like fire, hair, fur, rain. Particles can be
emitted from any kind of mesh object. The purpose of this video is
to acquaint you with the basic controls for a particle emitter.
We'll use the plane, which is the simplest to show. Switch to
animation view, with 100 frames.

1) Delete the default cube (Right click, then X, then confirm
delete). Add a plane (Space - Add - Mesh - Plane). Subdivide the
plane once (W key, then subdivide). Then go to the SR1-Animation
view.

2) Go to the Object buttons (F7), then click the Particles button,
all the way to the right. We will look at emitter type particles,
where the number of particles and their direction change over time.
Emitters are good for animating rain and fire, where raindrops and
smoke particles move over time. The hair type is for more static
simulations, like hair and fur.

3) Particles are emitted from faces of the plane. The default is
1000 particles over 100 frames = 10 particles per frame.

4) Increase the number of particles to 10000. You see that they're
emitting from each face by default. Can change to emit from
vertices, as well as volume.

5) Particles are most often emitted from the "normals", the direction that's perpendicular from the face. The Normals setting controls how high the particles are emitted. Set the normal to 1 to show how height is controlled. Press F12 to render.

6) Random adds a bit of randomness to the emitting direction. You can mix normals and random and press F12 to rendeer.

7) AccX, AccY, and AccZ can add an extra push in the respective direction. Set AccX to .5, which gives bias in the X direction of .5 Blender units. This is good for fire and smoke effects. Press ALT+A to see the path of the animation.

8) Emitting also works in negative direction. For rain, if you float a plane above the scene, and make it a particle emitter, this would be the start of a rain simulation. You can increase the randomness as well. Set Normals to -.5 and AccX to -.3. Properly textured, this could simulate a heavy rainstorm.

9) Start and End are the start and end frames for the particles. Life is how long the particle lives. Increasing the life makes the particles stay around longer. Start can be negative, which means that the particles are alive at the beginning of the animation.

Increase the life to 100. The particles stay around longer. For fireworks, you might want to vary the life and add some randomness to the emitter.

10) Start can be a negative number also. A negative start number means the simulation began before the first frame is rendered, like the fire is already going at frame 1.

11) Go to a frame 41 and press F12 to render. The particles render as halos, and the plane does not render. The emitter does not render by default.

12) Add a material, F5, shading, make the particles red (R=1, G=0, and B=0). Then press F12 render.

13) To change the halo effects, press the Halo button in the Render Pipeline panel. In the Shaders panel, you can change the halo size. You can also customize the halo - Rings, lines, stars.

Render (F12) for

1)   Halo with 4 rings and .5 size.

2)   Halo with size .1, 3 stars, and 4 lines

14)   Many material settings can be animated. Look at Halo Size. Go
to IPO window. Select the Material type curves. Then select HaSize.
Create an IPO curve, with CTRL+LMB, creating IPO points for size.
This creates a Bezier curve for the halo size, which will make them
emit with different sizes over time. Here's the resulting video.

These are the basic controls and look for emitter type particles,
which work well for fire and rain. We've barely scratched the
surface. I hope this gives you a good start towards understanding
Blender's particle system.

Soft Bodies (2.49)

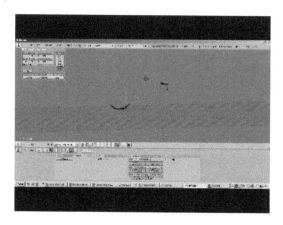

Watch the Video at: http://www.youtube.com/watch?v=jnu9rRlZt9M

Soft bodies are materials that have some flexibility, that can deform themselves when forces such as friction or gravity are applied to them. Soft body objects are common in real life. Think of clothing draped on a person or model, jello, rubber, or even metals under certain circumstances. They range in their degree of flexibility. You need to tweak the soft body settings to get the object to resemble the type of material you're trying to model. Rubber tires certainly doesn't deform in the same way as a balloon or a cape on Batman. In this tutorial, I will introduce you to the basic concepts behind soft body physics.

1) We're going to see how a soft body responds to gravity. Think of a towel swinging on a towel rack, affected by the wind and gravity. Start with default Blender scene. Go to Front View (NUM1). Delete default cube (Right Click to select, press DEL key, Enter to confirm). Add a grid (Space - Add - Mesh - Grid), with X Resolution and Y Resolution both at 20 Blender Units. Move the grid 4 or 5 Blender units up, in the blue Z direction. If the grid is in Object mode, Press Tab to go into Edit mode. Make sure all the vertices are selected. If not, press the A key.

2) Go to the Edit buttons (F9). The Soft Body physics requires that you create a vertex group consisting of all the vertices that will participate in the soft body simulation. In the Link and Materials panel, there is a group of buttons for creating vertex groups. Click the New button to make all the selected vertices (in this case, all the vertices in the grid) part of the vertex group called Group. Let's change the name to Softgroup (make sure the case matches exactly, with the name starting with a Capital S, and the rest of the

name in lower case). You can define more than one vertex group. For our purposes, we'll use only one.

The Weight refers to the default weight setting for each vertex in the group. We can change this later, when we weight paint the grid, so that certain vertices are not affected by the soft body physics, while others are. The default of 1 means that no vertices deform to the maximum soft body calculation. We'll do the opposite. Set the Weight to 0.00, and click on Assign. At this setting, all the vertices are affected by the Soft Body calculations.

3) What does this mean? Let's enable the Soft Body calculations. To do that, with the grid selected, tab into Object mode. Select the Object buttons (F7), and then click on the Physics buttons. Click the Soft Body button. Then click the Use Goal button. Click on the little icon with the up and down arrows to show that the Softgroup vertex group has been selected. That's it!

4) Navigate with either the middle mouse button or ALT+LMB, if your computer has the Emulate 3D Button Mouse button enabled in User Preferences, to give the view some downward perspective. To start the Soft Body animation, with the 3D Cursor in the 3D window, press ALT+A, or press SHIFT+ALT+A which will make the animation work in all windows. What happened? The object falls to the ground. Press ESC to stop the animation. It's affected by the Friction, Mass, Gravity, and Speed settings. In particular, the Gravity setting (9.8) has the most effect. 9.8 is the setting for earth's gravity, so the idea is that the object is falling onto the ground something like it would under earthlike conditions. If we set, say, Friction to a high number (change it to 5 from its default) and then press ALT+A to rerun the animation, the object falls to the ground a lot slower. The animation takes place over Blender's default of 250 frames, at 25 frames per second.

5) Not all of the vertices in the vertex group have to be affected by Soft Body physics. This happens a lot in real life. Think of a towel hanging on a towel rack, or a flag waving in the wind. The part of the towel or flag that's closest to the towel rack or flagpole stays still, while the rest of the towel or flag is affected. Painting the mesh to reflect realistically what moves and what does not move is key to making the soft body effect realistic. Blender's Weight Paint feature lets us do exactly that. To show how this works, go into Top view (NUM7). Then, switch to Weight Paint mode. Note how the grid turns all blue. Press the N key to access the Weight Paint properties panel. What this does is allow us to paint onto the mesh the areas we want affected by the Soft Body calculation. There's a color gradient between 0 and 1, blue standing for 0 and red standing for 1. Set the Weight to 1. You can set other parameters such as opacity and brush size, as well as blend

with the underlying mesh colors, but for now we'll keep it simple and just make the right corner not be affected by the soft body physics. Paint along the right corner of the grid. Note that it turns red.

Go into Front view (NUM1) and give the mesh some downward perspective as before. Start the animation (SHIFT+ALT+A). Now, instead of the soft body falling through the floor, the effect is more like a towel hanging on a towel rack, with the red area not moving and the blue area swinging.

6) Soft Bodies can interact with other objects in a realistic way. Let's add a sphere in an area that would be affected by the swinging soft body. Press SHIFT+C to position the 3D cursor at 0,0,0. Then add an icosphere (Space - Add - Mesh - Icosphere), accepting the defaults. Press ALT+A to animate. The soft body is not affected by the sphere, even though you would want the mesh to drape around the sphere somehow. To get that effect, select the icosphere, go to the Physics buttons, and click on Collision. Start the animation (SHIFT+ALT+A). The mesh now wraps around the icosphere, more or less as if a towel collided into a big ball while the towel was swinging in the wind. You can tweak the Inner, Outer, Absorption, and Damping settings to get the effect you want.

7) We can have a lot of fun with Soft Bodies. Let's delete the icosphere by selecting it, pressing the DEL key, and clicking Enter to confirm. Let's paint the left edge of the mesh red so that it isn't affected by Soft Body Physics. Again, go into Top view (NUM7) and make sure the weight is set to 1.0. Paint the left edge of the grid red. Press ALT+A to animate. Now the grid object behaves more like a hammock, motionless on the side, but responsive to gravity in between the sides.

8) Go back into Weight Paint. Let's paint the four corners red and the rest of the mesh blue. Change the gravity setting from 9.8 to - 9.8, to make the mesh respond as if it was pulled upwards by gravity. Press SHIFT+ALT+A to animate. Note how the effect is as if the mesh was blown upward, although anchored at the corners.

I hope you get the idea by now. There's a lot you can do with soft bodies. I hope you are inspired to experiment with this marvelous tool.

Exploding Ball Physics (2.49)

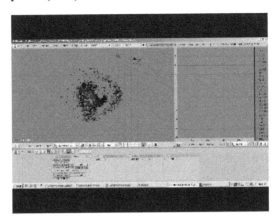

Watch the Video at: http://www.youtube.com/watch?v=dv4aIaIX2YA

You can do many interesting things with Blender's particle system. In addition to allowing meshes to emit particles (either dynamically with Emit or statically with Hair), one particle system can react to another particle system. This effect is called Reactor. In this tutorial, I will show you how to set up the effect of a glass ball being destroyed by a speeding bullet using both an emitter and reactor particle system.

Start with the default scene. Delete the default cube (Right click to select, press the DEL key, then press Enter to confirm the delete). Press Num1 to go to Front View. This way, Z is up and down, making your view the closest to the real world view. Turn off the 3D Transform widget, which gets in the way of the demonstration.

Add a UV Sphere (Space - Add - Mesh - UVSphere), accepting the default of 32 rings and 32 segments. For the purposes of this demo, the number of rings and segments doesn't matter. This will be the big glass ball that will be destroyed. Make it larger by scaling it 2 times (S - 2 - Enter). Go to the Shading buttons (F5) and add a material. Make it blue (R=0, G=0, B=1). Go to the Edit buttons (F9). Press the Set Smooth buttons to smooth out the ball.

Let's model the bullet. Position the 3D cursor 2 Blender Units in the X direction to the left of the UV Sphere. Add another UV Sphere, accepting the default. Rename the object from Sphere.001 to Bullet by going to the Object buttons and changing its name. This time, scale it down by .3 (S - .3 - Enter).

Add a particle system to the bullet by going to the Object buttons (F7) and clicking the Particle button. This will be an Emitter type particle system. Click the Random button to emit from random faces. Change the Normal velocity to 2. Change the visualization to Circle. Strictly speaking this not necessary, since we will remove the visualization when we obtain the final effect. You can tweak visualization and velocity to get the effect you want. Press ALT+A to watch the circular particles emanate from the sphere. Later on, this will be the path of the exploding fragments of the sphere as it is hit by the bullet. Press ESC to stop the animation.

Now select the big glass spherical ball. Add a particle system to it by pressing F7 and clicking the Particle button. This system will be a Reactor system. The particles are emitted in reaction to the activity of bullet's particle system. You specify the reactor object and its particle system index (starting from 1) in the Target: area. Type Bullet and accept 1, the first particle system on the bullet object. Note that you can have more than one particle system active on an object.

Make the following changes:

a) In the Basic: group, change the reaction type to Near. This makes the particles from the ball emit when the particles from the bullet are near the object.

b) Set Initial Velocity to 5 in the Normal direction and 5 in the Random direction.

c) Set AccZ to -9.8, which simulates the force of gravity downward, in the negative Z direction.

Let's animate the movement of the bullet through the sphere. Split the 3D window horizontally. Change the right window to an IPO Curve Editor window. Select the bullet, the small sphere. Press the I key to insert a location keyframe. Go to Frame 100. Position the bullet 2 Blender Units to the right, along the X axis (Press the G key, then X, then move the sphere along the axis). Press the I key to insert a location keyframe. In the IPO curve window click LocX. You can see the points representing the keyframes highlighted. LocY and LocZ haven't changed.

Go back to Frame 1. Press Shift-ALT+A to animate. The particles in the large sphere are emitted as the particles from the bullet approach the object.

Now for the magic. To make the big ball explode, add the Explode modifier. Go to F9 (Editing). Click Modifiers. Select Explode.

The explode modifier is added to the modifier stack. Press ALT+A to animate. The ball shreds into little pieces, into outer space in all directions.

We can simulate the pieces falling onto a flat surface. Position the 3D cursor under the spheres (in the -Z direction). Add a plane (Space - Add - Mesh - Plane). Scale it up 10 times (S - 10 - Enter). Press F7, the Object buttons. Go to the Physics buttons, the one in the middle of the second set of 3 buttons. Click the Collision button, which makes the particle system aware of the plane as a collision object. Press ALT+A to show how the plane now stops the partcles. You can play with the Particle Interaction settings, such as friction and damping.

Now that we have the effect the way we want it, it's time to stop showing the particles. That's easy. Select the small sphere. Go to the particles tab. Make Visualization None. Then Select the large sphere. Go to the Particles tab. Make Visualization None. Press ALT+A.

By the way, if you want to make a video out of this, be sure that you click the Render Emitter button in both particle systems. Otherwise you won't get either the bullet or the big ball to render.

Pretty neat! Now it's time for you to tweak the ball's destruction as you like.

Blender Game Engine (BGE)

BGE Animation Basics (2.49)

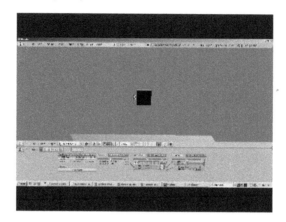

Watch the Video at: http://www.youtube.com/watch?v=UI_E_i8wENU

The purpose of this video is to compare animation in Blender 3D modeling with animation in the Blender Game Engine. The animation results are different because the BGE uses a different physics engine, Bullet Physics, than the 3D animation engine. As you will see, because the default frame rates are different, animations generated in the BGE are faster (60 frames per second) than in Blender 3D (25 frames per second). I will show how to visualize animations in both, how to synchronize the animations between the BGE and Blender 3D, and the basic visualization settings in the BGE that will let you fine tune your game animations.

I am using Blender 2.49b because, as far as I can tell, this is the only Blender version where you don't need Python scripting to synchronize the animations. Versions before 2.49 required you to have a Python script to set the default frame rate in the BGE. Blender 2.50, Alpha 0, has not fully implemented BGE animation yet. In 2.50 alpha 0, you can run a game and show visualizations, but you can't do animations in Blender 3D and have them show up in the BGE, or vice versa. Both of these can be done in 2.49b. I'll show you how to do both and why it's a good idea to be able to move smoothly back and forth between Blender 3D and the Blender BGE. So 2.49b seems to be the way to go if you want to do animation with the Blender Game Engine.

By the way, I have not seen this type of discussion anywhere, either as a video, in documentation, or in a book. The closest is Tony Mullen's book Bounce, Tumble, and Splash, which is an excellent introduction to Blender physics libraries such as the fluid simulator, soft bodies, cloth, boids, particles, and so on. However, he uses an older Blender version which needs a Python hack to synchronize the animation speeds between Blender 3D and the Blender BGE. My conclusions are the result of pure experimentation. If you have any comments on this, please join my Blender 3D forum at http://forum.irakrakow.com, and comment on this video.

Here are the steps:

a) Setup: Go into Animation View by selecting it from the different views available. Go into Front View, the best view for the BGE because of the gravity simulation, by pressing Num1 or View Front from the menu. Start by deleting the default cube (Select, right click, then confirm with the DEL key), Add an icosphere (Add - Mesh - Icosphere), accepting the defaults. Add a plane (Space - Add - Mesh - Plane). Tilt the plane 45 degrees (R - 45 - Enter) to tilt it. This will make the icosphere fall off the plane when we press P to play the game in the Blender Game Engine.

b) Before running the BGE, we need to make the icosphere an Actor, with rigid body physics. The plane will be an obstacle for the sphere, which will react according to gravity by falling off the plane. Movement of the sphere down the plane is dependent on gravity and the calculations of the Bullet Physics engine, as well as the mass of the object and other things. Press the P key with the 3D cursor in the 3D window to run the game. Press ESC to stop the game.

c) We can generate IPO curves from running the game. Check the Record Game Physics to IPO check box. Press the P key to run the game. Note how the IPO curves are generated in the IPO Curve Editor.

d) Here's how to fine tune collisions in the game engine. Select the icosphere. Select Bounds, and then Sphere. Check the Show Physics Visualization menu item from the Game menu. The visualization shows the rectangular area which is the collision area of the plane, as well as the spherical area which is the collision boundary for the sphere. This is how you check for valid collisions in the game engine. Press the P key to run the game. Press ESC to stop the game.

e) Let's see how our animation runs in the 3D part of Blender. Run the animation with ALT+A. Note how the animation runs much slower. Why is this? This is because the 3D animation is at 25 frames per

second. Go to Scene buttons and find the FPS indicator. The BGE
runs at 60 frames per second. In the World buttons, and this is ONLY
in 2.49, in the Mist/Stars/Physics panel, the Physics part refers to
the Blender Game Engine. The dropdown shows Bullet, the default
engine. There's also Servo Physics. We'll leave the engine at
Bullet. The FPS is at 60. We can change it to 25. Then rerun the
BGE by pressing the P key. Press the ESC key and new IPO curves are
generated.

f) We can also change Gravity. The default is earth's gravity at
9.8. Let's decrease it to 2, simulating a planet with less gravity.
Press the P key to rerun the BGE. Press ESC to end the game and
generate new curves.

g) We'll change gravity back to earth, 9.8. We're going to clear
out the IPO curves we created. Press the A key in the IPO Curve
Editor to select all the curves. Press the DEL key and confirm the
deletion.

Another way to generate IPOs, which bypasses actually running the
game, is to press CTRL+ALT+SHIFT+P with your objects in the position
as if you were going to run a game. Go to Frame 1. Position the
icosphere above the plane. Disable Record Game Physics to IPO in the
Game Menu. Instead, press CTRL+ALT+SHIFT+P. The Bullet Physics
engine runs, generating the IPO curves. Press ALT+A. Change gravity
to 16. Press CTRL+ALT+SHIFT+P. Then press ALT+A. We now have the
IPOs for gravity in a bigger planet, like Jupiter.

h) Let's go the other way, from 3D to the Game engine. We'll create
a simple animation in Blender 3D. First, get rid of the previous IPO
curves by going to the IPO Curve Editor, pressing the A key to select
all the curves, and pressing Delete. Set keyframes from 1 to 100.
Start with the ball. Keyframe it at Frame 1 by pressing the I key
and selecting LocRot. Go to Frame 100. Move it 5 or so Blender
Units up. Keyframe it by pressing the I key and selecting LocRot.
Press ALT+A. Now we have an animation in Blender 3D over 100 frames.

i) We can get the Blender Game Engine to run this animation using
Logic Bricks. Do the Always Sensor with the IPO actuator. Select
the Play type. Connect the sensor to the controller and the
controller to the actuator, as usual. Make the end frame the same as
the end frame in the 3D engine. Then run the BGE, to show that the
BGE can run the IPO curves created in the IPO Curve Editor.

I hope you now have a better idea of how animation works in Blender
3D as compared with the animation of the Blender Game Engine.

They're totally separate, yet, with more understanding of how Bullet Physics and gravity work, they can work well together.

Sensors and Actuators (2.49)

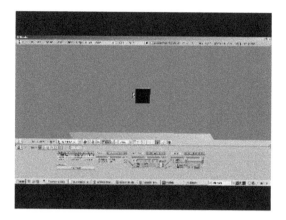

Watch the Video at: http://www.youtube.com/watch?v=AZwg8alNg5c

The purpose of this video is to show some basic sensor and actuator behavior. We'll look at the Always, Touch, and Keyboards sensors. I'll show you some basic techniques for moving an object, how the movement interacts with gravity, how to bounce an object, and how to replace one object with another object.

Setup:

We'll use the default cube. Go to Front View (NUM1), the best for the BGE because it shows the effect of gravity the best, as objects actually fall down in response to simulated gravity. Add a ground plane for the cube to bounce off of (Shift - Add - Mesh - Plane). Scale the plane 8 times (S - 8 - Enter). Move the plane down about 5 Blender Units. It doesn't really matter - you could have moved the cube up as well to get the same effect. Select the cube. Go to the Logic buttons (F4). Select Rigid Body from the Physics types dropdown. This turns on the Actor button as well, so that the cube becomes an actor, with the realistic Rigid Body physics applied, in the Game Engine.

Show:

1) The default sensor is the Always sensor. Click the Add buttons to add a Sensor, a Controller, and an Actuator, to the cube. Wire up the logic bricks, connecting the sensor to the controller and the controller to the actuator. Enter .10 in the LocX area. What this logic block is saying is that, each time the logic blocks are evaluated (the Always sensor - it's not strictly Always, it's when the logic is evaluated), the cube will be moved .10 Blender Units in the X direction. Press P to start the game. Note how the cube moves in the X direction (because of the logic brick), as well as

down (because of the rigid body physics) until it touches the plane (which is an obstacle that prevents the cube from falling any further). For a while, the cube moves in the X direction on the plane, until eventually it falls off the plane. Press ESC to end the game.

2) How to make the cube bounce. Enter 0 in the LocX area. Now enter .1 in the LocZ area, the third location area. Press P to start the game. Now, on every evaluation of the logic, the cube goes upward in the Z direction .1 Blender unit. At the beginning this causes the cube to go up a bit. Eventually, however, gravity takes over, being more powerful than the displacement in the Z direction, and the cube bounces down, until it hits the plane. After that, the cube bounces up in the Z direction, then gravity takes over, in an infinite cycle. Press ESC to stop the game.

3) Perhaps you want the cube to start bouncing only when it touches the ground, allowing gravity to control the cube fully before it hits the ground. To do that, change the Always sensor to a Touch sensor. Press the P key with the cursor in the 3D window to start the game. Note that the bounce doesn't take place until the plane touches the ground.

4) How to make the go in the X direction. Set the LocZ parameter back to 0. Set the LinV, linear velocity, to 0.10. This makes the cube's speed, in the X direction, become .10 Blender units, every time it touches the plane. The cube indeed goes into the X direction that way, but its motion is unrealistic because the cube seems to penetrate into the plane. Perhaps you can do better. Hint: a more realistic way is to use the Servo type of motion. Post your render at http://forum.irakrakow.com to show the cube moving more realistic, without going into the cube. Press ESC to end the game.

Now click the little Add button on the LinV row, at the right. What that does is add .10 Blender Units to the speed of the cube. It accelerates quickly along the X axis until it falls from the plane. Press ESC to end the game.

5) Here's an interesting effect. We can replace one mesh with another while the Game Engine runs. We'll use the Keyboard sensor to trigger this effect. We will replace the cube with Suzanne. Here's how it's done. Go to Level 2 by clicking on the second rectangle. Add Suzanne (Space - Add - Mesh - Monkey). Click back on Level 1. The Game Engine only shows the objects on Level 1. We'll substitute the cube with Suzanne when we hit the R key (for replace, I guess). First, change the Sensor to a Keyboard sensor by selecting Keyboard from the Sensor Type dropdown. Left click in the Key area. In the rectangle, where it says Press A Key, move the cursor. Then press

the R key. Now the key area displays the letter R. Whatever happens will be triggered when the user presses the R key.

In the Actuator area, select Edit Object. Below is a popup menu which lets you select the type of object editing you want. Select Replace Mesh. In the Obj: field, enter Suzanne. Wire the sensor to the controller and the controller to the actuator. Run the game by moving the cursor into the 3D window and pressing the P key. Press the R key. Suzanne magically replaces the cube. This is a great technique if, say, you want, say, your Cinderella mesh to be replaced by a pumpkin, as in the story. Press ESC to end the game.

6) Now suppose you want the cube back. We can show and hide the details about the sensor and actuator by clicking on the little arrow at the right. This is useful when you want to show a lot of logic bricks in a small area. So click these arrows to hide the details about the sensor and actuator. Let's make the C key restore the cube back. To do that, we need another set of logic bricks. Click the Add buttons on the Sensor, Controller, and Actuator tabs. Set the sensor type to Keyboard. Left click in the Key area. In the rectangle where it says Press a Key, press the C key. Now the key area displays the letter C.

In the Actuator area, select Edit Object. In the popup menu which lets you select the type of object editing you want, select Replace Mesh. In the Obj: field, enter Cube. Wire the sensor to the controller and the controller to the actuator. Run the game by moving the cursor into the 3D window and pressing the P key. Let the cube fall to the ground. Press the R key first, replacing the cube with the monkey. Press the C key next, replacing the monkey with te cube. Pretty neat...you can make objects appear and disappear.

One last thing I want to point out before my 10 minutes runs out. Don't worry. I'll show more stuff in the next part. It's a good idea to name your sensors something meaningful instead of Sensor and Sensor1, the default names. To do this, expand the details for each sensor. Name the first sensor Monkey. Then click the arrow to hide the details. Expand the details for the second sensor. Name the second sensor Cube. Now you can tell what each sensor does.

I hope this gives you a better idea of how to wire up logic bricks to do basic object movement, as well as how to replace one object with another under Game Engine control.

Falling Dominoes (2.49)

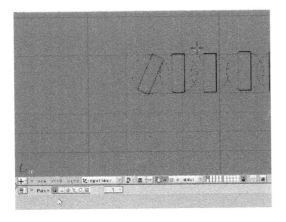

Watch the Video at: http://www.youtube.com/watch?v=ONrcGKcdnqE

If you are thinking about making a game in Blender, you will need to learn about Blender's special physics engine, Bullet Physics, as well as the game engine. Blender's physics makes the objects move more realistically. This tutorial touches both on the physics and the game engine, as well as showing you how to create a video of it.

So let's get started. Start up Blender with its default scene.

1) X erase the default cube. If object not selected navigate to it and right click to select.

2) Space Add Mesh Plane

3) S 5.

4) Left click object mode tab.

5) Space add mesh cube

6) tab object mode - S x make thinner.

7) S y make thinner.

8) Front view.

9) Z key - wire frame mode to see the plane.

10) Select the block - G move over to edge, close to plane.

11) Actor - Dynamic - Rigid Body - Bound - Box.

12) Domino - P key - goes to game engine.

13) Esc gets out of that.

14) Rotate the block a bit with R. with P falls over.

15) Duplicate these. Shift D across the plane.

16) You can texture these later. P key - they all fall over.

17) Get out of wire frame - solid mode.

18) Shift - D , rotate 90 - put it on top - make a building thing.

19) Then P key, they all fall over.

20) Alt A doesn't animate.

20) Then Game, Record Game Physics to IPO.

21) Alt - A then you can animate it.

22) Then you can create a movie out of it.

23) Scene F10.

24) Preview preset.

25) Quicktime.

26) ANIM button.

27) Output folder.

27) Falling domino video.

Hope you liked it. You can do a lot more - texture to make real
looking dominos, falling bricks with cubes stacked on top of each
other. You can be real destructive without, of course, having to
pick up the pieces. Enjoy!

Python

Blender Python User Interface, Part 1 (2.5)

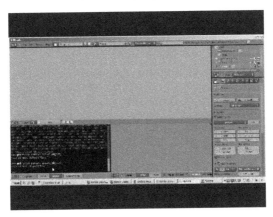

Watch the Video at: http://www.youtube.com/watch?v=vmhU_whC6zw

The purpose of this video is to give you an idea of the Python
scripting environment in the new Blender 2.5, as well as to give you
places to start if you either don't know Python at all, or are new to
programming. Don't be afraid if you are not a programmer. Python is
not a difficult language to learn. This tutorial is based on Blender
Labrat (mfoxdogg) tour of the Python setup in Blender 2.5, and the
Blender 2.5 Python API introduction at blender.org. I based this
tutorial on Blender 2.5 Alpha 1, released in mid-February, 2010.

The basic document is Blender 2.6 Python API (the Application
Programming Interface for Blender) document:
http://www.blender.org/documentation/250PythonDoc/contents.html

The Wiki page to start learning te Blender 2.5 Python API is at:
http://wiki.blender.org/index.php/Dev:2.5/Py/API/Intro

To learn Python itself, start at http://www.python.org and click the
Tutorials tab. You can do your learning entirely inside Blender,
using the new Python 3.1 console that's a part of Blender 2.5.

This API is undergoing modification. You're looking at the version
as of February 15, 2010. The basic module is bpy, which is a totally
different API than Blender 2.4x.

The functions are grouped into different types. For example, bpy.ops
documents the Blender Python operators. Under Mesh for example, you

can see the parameters for anything you can do with a mesh, in alphabetical order.

You can also access the API Reference from the Help Menu at any time.

2.5 has a number of pre-built setups for different purposes. By default, you start in the Default setup. For scripting, go to the menu of different setups and select Scripting.

There are a number of windows. We'll start with the Python 3.1 interactive console. This is a special Python console for Blender. The console already has imported the most used modules for Blender, such as bpy, bpy.data, bpy.ops, Mathutils, and so on. The standard Python 3.1 syntax will work here. You can learn Python itself just working with this console and reading the Python 3.1 documentation.

There are actually two consoles, Python (the default), and the Report Console, not discussed here. We'll use Autocomplete shortly.

If you have used an earlier version of Python, you will be shocked that if you enter:

```
print "Hello World"
```

you'll get an error message. That's because in Python 3.1, print is a function. You need to enter:

```
print("Hello World")
```

The console echoes your message, in blue.

Here's how Autocomplete can help you. Suppose you want to print all the objects in the scene. The object references are stored in bpy.data. When you don't know what properties are available, click the Autocomplete button). Try:

```
print(bpy.data.objects)
```

The Python console tells you that there are 3 objects, each stored as a collection. Python starts its index from 0. So:

```
print(bpy.data.objects[0])
```

prints "Camera"

```
print(bpy.data.objects[1])
```

prints "Cube"

```
print(bpy.data.objects[2])
```
prints "Lamp"

```
print(bpy.data.objects[3])
```
"Index 3 out of range" error message in pink

Suppose you want to know the location of the camera. Enter the following (hit autocomplate to find all the properties you can use):
```
print(bpy.data.objects[0].location)
```

The answer is a vector, with the x, y, and z location of the camera, in Blender Units.

Usually, you're not working with bpy.data, which is all the data in the file. Instead, you're most commonly working with the data that you can see, in your "context", so to speak.

For example, to find the name of the active object, type:

```
print(bpy.context.active_object)      (click on Autocomplate to see all
```
the properties you can find)
The console prints "Cube".

Just for fun, we'll change the active object by switching to the 3D window and selecting the Lamp. To do that, go to the Default setup, select the Lamp, go back to the Scripting setup, press Up arrow (the Up arrow lets you recall previous commands), and enter:
```
print(bpy.context.active_object)
```
The console prints "Lamp"

You can find the location of the lamp by entering:
```
print(bpy.context.active_object.location)
```
The console prints the lamp's location as a vector.

We can change the lamp's location by assigning it a new value. For example, let's change the lamp's z location (the indices are 0=x, 1=y, and 2=z) to 1
Enter the following:
```
bpy.context.active_object.location[2] = 1
```

Go back to the Default setup. Note that the lamp's z location is at 1 Blender unit, with the x and y coordinates unchanged.

Go back to the Scripting setup. Press the Up arrow in the Python console, recalling the print statement, to print the coordinates of the active object, and you'll see that what I said is true.

Now it's great that you have the Blender Python console. There's a lot more. You can load and run any Python script (with the .py extension), by going to the Text window, at the top, selecting Text - Open, and opening the file. Included in the zip file for 2.5 Alpha 1 are many scripts. They're either in the Python or Scripts folders. As a simple example, there are Template files included, which gives you a Python file with the basics filled in, so you can start programming more easily. In the Templates folder, under Scripts, is the file operator_simple.py. We'll load this into the text area.

In 2.5, everything is an operator. This is just a shell operator script, called "Simple Object Operator". By default, it just lists all the objects in the scene on the Blender console, which is what the code of the Main function does. If we press Alt-P or click Run Script, the script runs, and we've added this new operator. We'll look at the Blender console to see the output. We can search for our new Simple Object Operator, and even add it as a tool, if we go back to the Default setup. We just have to decide what Simple Object Operator is going to do. Just recode the Main function and run the script. If you register it, the script is loaded when you start up Blender.

This is just the first in a series on Blender Python programming. I hope you liked it.

Blender Python User Interface, Part 2 (2.5)

Watch the Video at: http://www.youtube.com/watch?v=ZAckF-o0qws

In Part 1 of this series on Blender 2.50 Python, we explored the new Blender 2.50 Python User Interface. In Part 2, we will look at the new user interface, consisting of windows and panels. You are already familiar with windows -- things like the 3D window, the Outline Window, and the UV / Image Editor Window. These still behave as 2.4x type windows, which you can resize, split, join, and so on.

However, the way windows are built is completely different. In Blender 2.5, windows are assembled in units called Panels. You program each panel as a Python class. A window is a group of panels, with each panel in the window registered to it. In this tutorial, we will explore how Blender 2.5 windows are put together by both looking at the scripts that build the windows in the user interface, and actually changing these windows. Then we will create a panel based on Blender's panel template script, and register it to a window, adding our own panel to a Blender window. In the process, we will see where the python scripts for the windows shipped with Blender are kept and examine how the user interface is created. The goal is to show you how to find the code for the windows, as a starting point for you to change the Python code to add panels to existing windows. The way of building the User Interface has changed so much in 2.50 that just about all Blender Python 2.4x scripts that use windows need to be rewritten, basically from the ground up.

This tutorial is based on the Blender 2.5 Tour 9, Python tutorial, by Michael Fox (mfoxdogg), at: http://mfoxdogg.com/2_5_tour_python.ogg.

So start up Blender 2.5 Alpha 1. The 3D window has a default cube. We won't be doing anything with any Blender objects in this tutorial. We'll only be looking at the user interface scripts. First off, where are they? To find out, switch the 3D window to a Text window by going to the window type buttons menu. The text icon is the same as in Blender 2.4x. From the Text menu, select Open. Bundled into the distribution files is a .blender folder. It may be hidden on your computer, so enable unhiding folders in your operating system, if you don't see that folder. The Blender Python scripts are in the Scripts folder. By the way, there are other Python scripts in the Python/lib folder. You can look at these, which are part of the Python 3.1 distribution, to learn more about Python itself. Today, we're going to look at the Scripts folder.

The Scripts folder itself contains a number of folders: extensions, IO, modules, op, presets, templates, and ui. We're going to start by going to the ui folder, which contains the scripts for the windows in Blender's user interface. The script names start with either "properties_" or "space_". The ones starting with "properties_" are the scripts for the various properties windows. The scripts starting with "space_" are scripts for Blender's windows, such as console, dopesheet, and 3D. Space_view3d.py, for example, is the script for the 3D window.

We're going to start with the script for the Material window, properties_material.py. In the window on the far right, which you may need to expand a bit, click on the big spherical icon. This is the Material window, which is the window produced by this script. The window is divided into sections, which are coded as Property panels. Hide the details of each panel, so that only the headers -- things like Preview, Diffuse, Specular and so on -- show.

Corresponding to each of these panels is a Python class of starting with the words MATERIAL_PT. In the code, the panels are not coded in the order that you see them. In fact, there are panels that you don't see. The panel for the Diffuse settings is labeled "Diffuse", and the code to build the user interface elements, such as the list of shaders, is in the class called MATERIAL_PT_diffuse, specifically in the Draw function, which is required for any panel, some of the code of which is highlighted in pink. There's a class called MATERIAL_PT_specular for the specular panel, with its Draw function, a class called MATERIAL_PT_shading for the Shading panel, and so on.

All the way at the bottom is a list of the panel classes in this window, which are highlighted. This is the order that the panels will display in, although not all of them may display. These classes are registered when the register function, highlighted here, is called. Note that the Physics panel is not displayed. That's because Physics is not appropriate to the Blender Render material window. However, if we switch to Blender Game, where Physics is relevant, the panel displays. In the code for the Physics panel, we see that the panel only should display for the Blender Game engine.

One last thing. The material window class has the following properties:
```
 bl_space_type = 'PROPERTIES'
    bl_region_type = 'WINDOW'
    bl_context = "material"
```

Remember this when we build our panel, to add to the Material window. To build a panel, Blender has a template script called panel_simple.py, in the Templates folder. This script, by default, adds a "Hello World" panel, which displays the active object name, to the Object panel. Since we want to add this panel to the material window, we change bl_context to "material". The draw function actually draws the layout on the panel. The row() function creates a row. Three rows are created, one of which displays "Hello World" with an icon. The second row displays the name of the active object. The third row is an input area where we can change the name of the cube.   Finally, this new class is registered.

If we press the Run Script button, the script runs. Look at the Material window. The Hello World panel was added at the bottom. Change the name of the cube to MyCube. Look in the outliner. The name of the object has changed.

Of course, there's a lot more, such as the details of how panels are drawn. We'll leave that for another tutorial. For now, I hope you have a better idea of how the new 2.5 interface works and how the scripts are organized.

Python 3 Assignment Statement (2.5)

Watch the Video at: http://www.youtube.com/watch?v=PBtJGgskrEU

The goal of this tutorial is to introduce Blender users, whether or not they are programmers, to Python 3. Blender 2.5 supports Python 3 scripts, which can let you program Blender behavior very precisely. Of course, before you can create Blender scripts, you need to know Python 3. We will use the Blender 2.5 Scripting environment, which includes a Python console that supports most (but not all) of Python 3, as well as a fully featured text editor, with advanced features such as autocomplete and automatic indenting of code. I will point out where Blender's Python implementation differs from the standard Python 3 distribution. There are minor differences, none that should prevent you from writing fully featured scripts in Blender 2.5.

Before working through the examples in this tutorial, you need to download Blender 2.5. You can do this at:
http://www.blender.org/download/get-25-alpha/

This series is based on the Python 3 tutorial, at:
http://docs.python.org/dev/3.0/tutorial/. It is not meant to cover all aspects of Python 3. I will cover enough so that you should be able to write Python scripts in Blender 2.5. This tutorial, the first in my Python 3 Programming series, will cover the Blender 2.5 Python console, how to create simple expressions and assignments, and how to use the Python 3 console as a calculator. We'll go into more depth in further tutorials.

So let's get started. Start up Blender 2.5. I'm using the version most current, which is Blender 2.5, Alpha 2. We're not going to be doing any 3D modeling or game design. Instead, we'll go to the Scripting setup, which you can select from the dropdown at the top row. Place the cursor in the lower left window, the Python console, and press control-down arrow to make it full screen. This is where we will stay.

First, note the 3 greater than signs (>>>). This is the Python console prompt. As you type, make sure that the cursor is inside the console window. Otherwise, what you type won't print.

From the console, we can enter a line of Python code and see it run. We'll write the traditional first line of code, which prints "Hello World" on the console.

>>>print("Hello World")

Hello World

On the console is the text Hello World, in blue. Congratulations,
you have written your first Python script.

Note that you need to enclose what you want to print in parentheses.
This differs from earlier Python versions, notably the Python 2
version that is included with Blender 2.4x, which did not require the
parentheses. Let's type what would have worked in Python 2 (and
Blender 2.4x), and see what happens.

```
>>>print "Hello World"
 File "<string>", line None
SyntaxError: invalid syntax (<console>, line 1)
```

This is the Python console's way of telling you that you made a
coding syntax error. The message is a bit mysterious. What Python
is trying to tell you is that there was an error, on line 1 (the only
line in the code), and that there's something wrong with the string.
At this point, just remember that you need the parentheses for the
print statement.

In Python, a string like "Hello World" can get assigned to a
variable. To assign the variable x to "Hello World", enter:

```
>>>x = "Hello World"
>>>
```

It appears that nothing happened. You get the >>> prompt again. But
actually, space to hold the contents of the variable x was created in
memory, and the variable x was assigned the string "Hello World"

Now, instead of printing the string, you can print the variable
contents, as follows:

```
>>>print(x)
Hello World
```

There are rules for variable names. One is that the variable name
must start with a letter. Let's see what happens when we try to
print the contents of the variable y.

```
>>>print(y)
Traceback (most recent call last):
   File "<console>", line 1, in <module>
NameError: name 'y' is not defined
```

This time, Python tells us that the name y is not defined. So if you want Python to print the contents of a variable, it needs to be assigned, as x was. By the way, you don't need to code the print() function (that's what the parentheses mean) if you want to print the contents of a variable. You can simply enter it. Just enter:

```
>>>x
'Hello World'
```

The single quotes around the contents of x indicates that inside is the contents of the variable x.

Python variable names are case sensitive, which means that capitalization counts. So entering:

```
>>>print(X)
Traceback (most recent call last):
   File "<console>", line 1, in <module>
NameError: name 'X' is not defined
```

produces another NameError message. In the Python world, these error messages are called Exceptions. We'll talk about Exceptions in a later tutorial in more detail. For now, it's Python's way of saying you made a mistake.

If you enter a number (a whole number or decimal), Python treats just as if you entered it in your calculator. So you can enter:

```
>>>5 * 9
45
```

Python calculates the answer, just as if you entered the numbers in a calculator. You can use the standard symbols, +, -, / , and *, as well as ** for power.

There are other symbols. I'll point out an interesting one related to division. If you type:

```
>>>5 / 3
1.6666666666666667
```

This is the standard division symbol. The // is called integer division. If you type:

```
>>> 5 // 3
1
```

you get just the integer part of the division. If you do a "no no" like dividing by zero, for example:

```
>>> 5 / 0
Traceback (most recent call last):
  File "<console>", line 1, in <module>
ZeroDivisionError: int division or modulo by zero
```

you get another error message, ZeroDivisionError

Refer to the Python 3 documentation, at http://www.python.org, for more symbols, which are called operators.

The pound sign (#) is a comment. Comments document your code. Anything after the # is ignored. You'll see why comments are important when you write larger programs than one liners, in the text editor. You can enter:

```
>>>x    # this is a comment
'Hello World'
```

The text after the comment is ignored. Entering just a comment

```
>>># this is another comment
>>>
```

Once you assign a value to a variable, you can use it. Here's an example:

```
>>> width = 20
>>> height = 5*9
>>> width * height
900
```

A value can be assigned to several variables simultaneously:

```
>>> x = y = z = 20
>>> x
20

>>> y
20

>>> z
20
```

A special character, the underscore (_), prints the last calculation. Thus:

```
>>> x * 5
100
>>> _
100
```

There are some special functions that relate to numbers. For example, you can use the round() function to round a number or expression to a specific number of decimal places.

```
>>> round(3.141592222,4)
3.1416
```

We covered a lot of ground. We were introduced to the Python console, how to print literal strings and assign them to variables, how the Python console behaves when there's an error, and how to use Python as a calculator. In the next tutorial, we'll go into more detail about string handling, a key part of Python programming.

Python 3 Strings (2.5)

Watch the Video at: http://www.youtube.com/watch?v=geoly0UNCvA

In Part 1 of this series, we saw how to use Blender's Python 3 console, as well as how to write simple one line programs and make variable assignments. In this tutorial we are going to dig deeper in strings, arguably the most important type of variable in Python. We'll discover how to write strings, what happens when strings become very long or span more than one line, and how to use operators to combine strings or to make multiple copies of the same string text.

There's a lot to talk about. So without further ado, lets begin.

So, as in Part 1, start up Blender. I'm using the latest version, as of this video date, Blender 2.5, Alpha 2. Go to the Scripting setup. With the cursor on the Python console, press Control-Down Arrow to maximize the Python 3 console. We're ready to enter some strings to see the different ways they can be entered.

A string can be enclosed in single quotes:

```
>>>'spam eggs'
'spam eggs'
```

Or it can be entered enclosed in double quotes:

```
>>>"spam eggs"
'spam eggs'
```

You get the same result either way. Note that the string is echoed enclosed in single quotes, no matter which way you entered.

Suppose you make the leftmost quote a double quote and the rightmost quote a single quote:

```
>>>"spam eggs'
File "<string>", line None
SyntaxError: EOL while scanning string literal (<console>, line 1)
```

That's an error. Use either both single quotes or both double quotes.

What if there's a single quote inside the string. Entering:

```
>>>doesn't
  File "<string>", line None
SyntaxError: invalid syntax (<console>, line 1)
```

also produces a syntax error. You have one of two ways of solving this. You could use double quotes instead:

```
>>>"doesn't"
"doesn't"
```

or you can use what's called an escape character, the backslash (\), before the apostrophe, as in:

```
>>>'doesn\'t'
"doesn't"
```

What the escape character does is treat the second apostrophe, not as the end of the string, but as an actual apostrophe. You can escape the double quote the same way:

```
>>>"doesn\"t"
'doesn"t'
```

If you want to assign a long string, one longer than fits in one line, the backslash has another meaning: there's more to this string. Here's an example. Enter:

```
hello = "This is a rather long string containing\
...
```

What do those 3 dots mean? They mean that the console is asking for the next part of thne string. So enter:

```
...the next line of text."
```

Now enter:

```
>>>print(hello)
This is a rather long string containing the next line of text
```

Suppose you want the first part of the string to print on one line and the second part to print on the other. Use \n to indicate a new line. Enter the following:

```
>>> hello = "This is a rather long string containing \n \
...      the second line of text"
>>> print(hello)
This is a rather long string containing
      the second line of text
```

Note that the second line is indented. White space, or spaces, count as a character.

There's a special significance to matching triple quotes """ or mathching triple apostrophes. What's entered between them prints, with the spacing preserved, without you having to enter all those bothersome escape sequences. Thus:

```
>>>print ( """
...  hello my name is
...      Ira
... """)

 hello my name is
     Ira
```

Strings can be combined using the + operator. Python is smart enough to see that when the + operator is used for 2 strings, it doesn't add the strings, as it would for numbers. Instead, it combines them. To produce my full name from my first and last name, enter:

```
>>> fullname = "Ira" + "Krakow"
>>> fullname
'IraKrakow'
```

To add a space between my first and last name, simply add a space at the beginning of my last name.

```
>>> fullname = "Ira" + " Krakow"
>>> fullname
'Ira Krakow'
```

Mixing strings and numbers when combining (the technical term is concatenating), is a no-no. Entering:

```
>>> 2 + 'Ira'
Traceback (most recent call last):
  File "<console>", line 1, in <module>
TypeError: unsupported operand type(s) for +: 'int' and 'str'
```

produces an exception, a "TypeError", trying to mix a number and a string.

However, enclosing the 2 in quotes (either single or double), works because now '2' is a string

```
>>> 'ira' + '2'
'ira2'
```

The * operator repeats a string some number of times. Entering:

```
>>> 'ira'*3
'irairaira'
```

repeats my name 3 times.

If you omit the operator, concatenating is assumed. Thus:

```
>>> 'ira' 'krakow'
'irakrakow'
```

This concludes Part 2 of the Python 3 tutorial. We've gone more in depth about assigning a variable to a string, how to enter multi line strings, and how to combine and replicate strings. In Part 3 we'll

Python 3 Lists (2.5)

Watch the Video at: http://www.youtube.com/watch?v=SH0L3qjHdyw

In Part 2, we saw different ways that string variables can be defined. In this tutorial, we will see how lists of variables can be defined and used. You're basically creating more than one variable at a time, in a structure called a list. Lists are a very important part of Python. If you want to be able both program in Python and to read Python code written by others, you need to know how lists work. Don't worry, you'll get the hang of it if you practice a bit.

As before, start Blender 2.5. We will be using the Python console for the most current version, 2.5 Alpha 2. Go to the Scripting setup. Position the cursor in the Python console window, at the lower left corner, and press control-down arrow to maximize the window.

In Python, if a variable is assigned to a value that is enclosed in single quotes or double quotes (x = 'Hello' or x = "Hello"), then it's assumed to be a string. If the variable is assigned to a number, either a whole number or one with a decimal component, like x = 2, the variable is numeric. You can add, subtract, multiply, and divide. The most recent assignment of a variable determines how it is used.

Here's how it works:

```
>>> x = "Hello"
>>> y = "World"
>>> x + y
'HelloWorld'
```

Since x and y are enclosed in double quotes, Python interprets them as strings. The + operator for strings concatenates them, produciint 'HelloWorld'.

```
>>> x = 2
>>> y = 2
>>> x + y
4
```

go into even greater depth, as we look at how to slice and dice strings into substrings, as well as how to create lists.

Now, x and y are redefined as numbers. The + operator now adds them, producing the answer 4. Python won't allow numbers and strings to be added. So:

```
>>> x = "World"
>>> x + y
Traceback (most recent call last):
  File "<console>", line 1, in <module>
TypeError: Can't convert 'int' object to str implicitly
```

produces an error message.

With a list, you can define and work with lists of variables at once. Variables in a list are enclosed in square brackets []. You can mix strings and numbers in the list.

Let's start with a list, x, containing 4 variables, 2 strings and 2 numbers

```
>>> x = ['corned', 'beef', 555, 666]
>>>
```

Each variable in the list is called an element. Python has an interesting numbering system for list elements. It starts numbering from 0. So:

```
>>> x[0]
'corned'

>>> x[1]
'beef'

>>> x[2]
555

>>> x[3]
666
```

You can use the + operator on list elements the same way as if they were variables. Thus:

```
>>> x[0] + x[1]
'cornedbeef'
```

The first two elements are concatenated, since they are strings.

```
>>> x[2] + x[3]
1221
```

The first two elements are added, since they are numbers.

But:

```
>>> x[1] + x[2]
Traceback (most recent call last):
  File "<console>", line 1, in <module>
TypeError: Can't convert 'int' object to str implicitly
```

produces an error because Python doesn't know how to add 'beef' to 555.

Python also knows how to count backwards, from the end of the list. The last element of a list has the index -1, the next to last element has the index -2, and so on.

```
>>> x[-1]
666
```

```
>>> x[-2]
555
```

```
>>> x[-3]
'beef'
```

```
>>> x[-4]
'corned'
```

The + operator works with negative indices just as with positive indices.

```
>>> x[-1] + x[-2]
1221
```

```
>>> x[-3] + x[-4]
'beefcorned'
```

If you want to know how many elements are in a list, use the len()
function. Python provides many functions to save you the time and
effort of writing a program to find out frequently needed
information. We'll talk about functions in a future video.

```
>>> len(x)
4
```

You can change a list element. Thus:

```
>>> x[0] = 'roast'
>>> x
['roast', 'beef', 555, 666]
```

changed the first element from 'corned' to 'roast'.

```
>>> x[3] = x[3] * 3
>>> x
['roast', 'beef', 555, 1998]
```

multipled the fourth element (666) by 3.

```
>>> x[1] = x[1] + x[0]
>>> x
['roast', 'beefroast', 555, 1998]
```

concatenated the changed the second element from 'beef' to
'beefroast'.

If an element does not exist, Python produces an error message.
Thus:

```
>>> x[4]
Traceback (most recent call last):
   File "<console>", line 1, in <module>
IndexError: list index out of range
```

There is no x[4]. There are only 4 elements (remember, we count from 0). x[4] attempts to reference the fifth element in the list.

When we worked backward, remember that we started from -1. So:

```
>>> x[-4]
'roast'
```

However, trying to reference the fifth element, counting backwards, as in:

```
>>> x[-5]
Traceback (most recent call last):
   File "<console>", line 1, in <module>
IndexError: list index out of range
```

produces an error message.

You can define an empty list, with no elements, if you define just the square brackets with nothing between them.

```
>>> x= []
>>> x[0]
Traceback (most recent call last):
   File "<console>", line 1, in <module>
IndexError: list index out of range
```

x is a list with no elements. Trying to access the first element in the list produces an error.

That's it. I hope you enjoyed this introduction to lists. There are many situations where handling groups of variables in a list will make our programming much easier. In the next part, when we discuss slicing, you'll discover even more ways that Python can handle groups of variables easily.

Python 3 Slicing (2.5)

Watch the Video at: http://www.youtube.com/watch?v=ylyc1UFE3VM

In Part 3, we were introduced to lists, which lets us work with more than one variable at once. We also saw how to reference parts of the list, say the 3rd element in the list x as x[2] (since we start numbering from 0), using the [] operator, and how to use negative numbers to reference list elements from the end. In this tutorial, we will go into more detail about how to get parts of strings and lists, by use of slicing. Slicing also uses the square brackets, but in a new and different way.

As usual, start Blender 2.5. We will be using the Python console for the most current version, 2.5 Alpha 2. Go to the Scripting setup. Position the cursor in the Python console window, at the lower left corner, and press control-down arrow to maximize the window.

First, we'll look at slicing up strings. We'll start by working with the string 'Happy Blendering' You can use the same [] operator on strings that you can use with lists.
Thus:

```
>>> s = 'Happy Blendering'
```

The index numbering starts at 0.

```
>>> s[0]
'H'
```

The last element is referenced by -1.

```
>>> s[-1]
'g'
```

For this purpose, think of a string as a list of characters.

What if you wanted to extract a part of a string, for example, the word "Happy"? This is where slicing comes into play. The slice operator uses the colon to extract a range of characters in a string, with a bit of a twist. The number to the left of the colon is the starting position, and the number to the right of the colon is the ending position, MINUS ONE. You might think that if you enter:

```
>>> s[0:4]
'Happ'
```

you would retrieve the entire word Happy. Instead, you get just "Happ", the first four letters. You need to enter:

```
>>> s[0:5]
'Happy'
```

The rule is that to find the number of characters you'll get back, subtract the number to the right of the colon (5) by the number to the left of the colon (0). So:

```
>>> s[1:2]
'a'
```

'a' is the second letter (s[1]), but the length is only one character, stopping at s[2].

If the second number is equal or less than the first number, and both numbers are positive, the null string is returned:

```
>>> s[2:1]
''
```

If we omit the number after the colon, the rest of the string, from that point, is returned.

```
>>> s[1:]
'appy Blendering'
```

On the other hand, if we omit the number before the colon, the start point is the beginning of the string.

```
>>> s[:5]
'Happy'
```

which is the same as:

```
>>> s[0:5]
'Happy'
```

If you omit both the beginning and ending elements numbers, you get the whole string. That makes sense, start at the beginning and end at the end.

```
>>> s[:]
'Happy Blendering'
```

How do we get the word "Blendering"? If you try:

```
>>> s[-10:-1]
'Blenderin'
```

you miss the last letter. That scan started from the 10th letter from the end (the B) and ended, but did not include, the last letter (the G). Remember that the last element is not returned. To get it, omit the -1.

```
>>> s[-10:]
'Blendering'
```

There's a third parameter. If you add another colon, you can get "every nth" element. So:

```
>>> s[::2]
'HpyBedrn'
```

skips every other letter. Or,

```
>>> s[::3]
'HpBnrg'
```

returns the first, fourth, seventh, etc. elements.

As I said, strings behave almost like lists. The one area where a
lists behaves different from a string is that a string cannot be
changed. So if you try to insert a string, as in:

```
>>> s[5] = "Python"
Traceback (most recent call last):
  File "<console>", line 1, in <module>
TypeError: 'str' object does not support item assignment
```

you get an error message.

You can concatenate sliced strings together using the + operator.
Here's how to create the string "Happy Python Blendering"

```
>>> t = s[:5] + ' Python ' + s[-10:]
>>> t
'Happy Python Blendering'
```

Slices can be used with lists.

```
>>> s = ['The','quick','brown','fox']
>>> s
['The', 'quick', 'brown', 'fox']
```

Using the [-1:] notation, you can add more elmeents to the end of the
list.

```
>>> s[-1:] = ['jumped','over','the','lazy','dog']
>>> s
['The', 'quick', 'brown', 'jumped', 'over', 'the', 'lazy', 'dog']
```

To insert a list element before the nth element use the [n:n]
notation, as follows:

```
>>> s[1:1] = ['very']
>>> s
['The', 'very', 'quick', 'brown', 'jumped', 'over', 'the', 'lazy',
'dog']
```

Use the empty element, assigning to a slice, to delete a range of elements. This will delete the 2nd, 3rd, and 4th elements in the list.

```
>>> s[1:4] = []
>>> s
['The', 'jumped', 'over', 'the', 'lazy', 'dog']
```

The tuple is a cousin of the list. Just assign a comma separated set of values to a variable. A tuple prints in parentheses. It behaves exactly like a list in terms of slices. For example:

```
>>> s = 2, 100, 'ira'
>>> s
(2, 100, 'ira')
```

```
>>> s[1:2]
(100,)
```

```
>>> s[1:3]
(100, 'ira')
```

However, like a string (and unlike a list), you cannot change a tuple element. The following produces an error.

```
>>> s[1:3] = 'eduardo'
Traceback (most recent call last):
  File "<console>", line 1, in <module>
TypeError: 'tuple' object does not support item assignment
```

That's the basics of slicing, an efficient way to create substrings or parts of lists or tuples.

Python 3 List Methods (2.5)

Watch the Video at: http://www.youtube.com/watch?v=_HjITxJvLWQ

We saw how to use slicing to work with parts of a string, list, or
tuple, as well as how to insert, delete, and add to these types of
variables. Python has a number of built in methods -- also called
functions -- that can do these operations in a way that makes the
code easier to read. Sometimes it's a bit hard to understand all
those colons and square brackets, and it's easier to use words like
append, remove, or insert, which are, indeed the names of methods
associated with lists. We'll also see how these easy to understand
methods can be used to build a simple stack (where the last element
added is the first element retrieved) or queue (where the first
element added is the first element retrieved). We'll also discover
how to sort, count, and locate items in a list. Along the way, we'll
learn about the autocomplete feature of Blender's Python console, a
handy feature that documents available methods.

We'll be working in the Python 3 console window again. So start
Blender 2.5. We will be using the Python console for the most
current version, 2.5 Alpha 2. Go to the Scripting setup. Position
the cursor in the Python console window, at the lower left corner,
and press control-down arrow to maximize the window.

First off, what is a method, anyway? In Python, a list is actually
an object. Depending on the type of object, Python defines methods,
which are actions that can be done with the object. The Python
console's AutoComplete feature displays a list of what can be done
with the particular type of object.

Start with a string object. Enter:

>>> s = 'happy blendering'

which is a string. Then type
>>> s.

and press the Autocomplete button. You get a list of different
things you can do with the string s.

capitalize(center(count(encode(endswith(expandtabs(find(
format(index(isalnum(isalpha(isdecimal(isdigit(
isidentifier(islower(isnumeric(isprintable(isspace(istitle(
isupper(join(ljust(lower(lstrip(maketrans(partition(

```
replace(  rfind(  rindex(  rjust(  rpartition(  rsplit(  rstrip(
split(  splitlines(  startswith(  strip(  swapcase(  title(
translate(  upper(  zfill(
```

Let's use the capitalize() method to capitalize the first letter of
the string.

```
>>> s = 'happy blendering'
>>> s.capitalize()
'Happy blendering'
```

Sometimes, a method produces a True/False results, like you're asking
the string a question. For example, a numeric string is a string
that consists of numbers. Right now, s does not have that quality.
So entering:

```
>>> s.isnumeric()
False
```

However, assigning a numeric value to the string s, and asking if it
is numeric, would produce a True result.

```
>>> s = '3452'
>>> s.
capitalize(  center(  count(  encode(  endswith(  expandtabs(  find(
format(  index(  isalnum(  isalpha(  isdecimal(  isdigit(
isidentifier(  islower(  isnumeric(  isprintable(  isspace(  istitle(
isupper(  join(  ljust(  lower(  lstrip(  maketrans(  partition(
replace(  rfind(  rindex(  rjust(  rpartition(  rsplit(  rstrip(
split(  splitlines(  startswith(  strip(  swapcase(  title(
translate(  upper(  zfill(
>>> s.isnumeric()
True
```

Let's redefine s to be a list instead of a string. Enter:

```
>>> s = ['mary','had','a','lamb']
```

Then, enter the following and click the Autocomplete button.
```
>>> s.
```

```
append( count( extend( index( insert( pop( remove( reverse(
sort(
```

You get an entirely different set of methods, things you can do with
a list. Methods are functions that can be done, depending on the
type of data.

Let's look at these list-specific methods in more detail.

The append() method has a string argument (what you put between the
parentheses and will add it to the end of the list. Thus:

```
>>> s.append('and')
>>> s
['mary', 'had', 'a', 'lamb', 'and']
```

append() adds just one item to the list. If you want to add more
than one item, instead of using multiple append() statements, you can
use the extend() method, to extend the list with a list of values.
Here's an example:

```
>>> s.extend(['a','dog'])
>>> s
['mary', 'had', 'a', 'lamb', 'and', 'a', 'dog']
```

Note how extend() requires a list argument, while append requires a
string argument.

insert() inserts an item at a given position, or index. Remember, we
start counting from 0. If we wanted to insert the word 'large' in
front of the word 'dog' (the 7th word), we would enter:

```
>>> s.insert(6,'large')
>>> s
['mary', 'had', 'a', 'lamb', 'and', 'a', 'large', 'dog']
```

To remove an item from the list, use remove(), specifying the value
of the item to be removed. To remove the word 'large', the one we
just inserted, enter:

```
>>> s.remove('large')
```

```
>>> s
['mary', 'had', 'a', 'lamb', 'and', 'a', 'dog']
```

The pop() method, with no arguments, returns the last item in the list AND deletes it from the list. So:

```
>>> t = s.pop()
>>> t
'dog'
```

```
>>> s
['mary', 'had', 'a', 'lamb', 'and', 'a']
```

To implement a last in first out stack, add to the stack with append() and remove it from the stack with pop(). If you want a last in first out queue, use pop(0) instead of pop() and the first element will be removed.

pop() can take an argument, which is the index of the value to pop. So:

```
>>> s.pop(4)
'and'
```

```
>>> s
['mary', 'had', 'a', 'lamb', 'a']
```

Thus, the fifth word ('and') was removed.

The index(string) method returns the index number of the first occurrence of the string. Suppose we want to find the string 'lamb' in the list s, delete it from s, and assign it to t. You could do it this way:

```
>>> t = s.pop( s.index('lamb') )
>>> t
'lamb'
```

```
>>> s
['mary', 'had', 'a', 'a']
```

The count(value) method returns the number of times the value occurs in the list. Thus:

```
>>> s.count('a')
2
```

The sort() method does what it says, sorting the list, from lowest to highest value. Thus

```
>>> s.sort()
>>> s
['a', 'a', 'had', 'mary']
```

The reverse() methods sorts the list from highest to lowest value. Thus:

```
>>> s.reverse()
>>> s
['mary', 'had', 'a', 'a']
```

To summarize, we've been introduced to the autocomplete feature, which shows the methods available for particular object types, we explored the methods available for the list object, and in the process we have seen how to implement a stack (last in first out) and a queue (first in first out).

Python 3 Functions (2.5)

Watch the Video at: http://www.youtube.com/watch?v=UPhRBxrvW8w

In this tutorial, we are going to see how to write and call functions
in Python 3, as well as how to pass arguments, both as keyword and
value, to a Python function. I will also introduce you to some of
the neat features of the Blender 2.5 text editor, such as source code
color coding, which help make coding Python scripts much easier.
This video is based on the Python 3.1 function tutorial at:
http://docs.python.org/release/3.0.1/tutorial/controlflow.html#more-
on-defining-functions.

So start Blender 2.5. We'll be using the most current version, 2.5
Alpha 2. Go to the Scripting setup. Up to now, we've been using the
console window, in the lower left corner. In this video, we'll be
using the text editor window, in the upper left corner. Position the
cursor in the Python text editor window, and press control-down arrow
to maximize the window.

I pasted into the text editor window the code for the function to
find all the Fibonacci numbers up to a given positive whole number n.
The function is called fib(n) and the code is shown below:

```
def fib(n):     # write Fibonacci series up to n
    """Print a Fibonacci series up to n."""
    a, b = 0, 1
    while b < n:
        print(b, end=' ')
        a, b = b, a+b
    print()
```

When you paste code in Blender's text editor, all the code is in
black. There is no syntax highligting or line numbering. To turn on
line numbering, click the first icon on the left. This shows line
numbers to the left of the text. This is a handy feature, because
when an error occurs, Python will tell you the line number at which
the error occurred. Turning on syntax highlighting will highlight
things like comments (in green), keywords (in purple), numeric
constants (in blue), and function definitions (in gold).

In Python 3, the def keyword precedes the function definition, in
this case fib(), with n as the argument. You need the colon to
define the end of the function definition. A comment, in green,

tells us what the fib() function does. There's also a docstring, intended to be a larger comment, that is highlighted in red. Docstrings start with three double quotes and end with three double quotes.

The Fibonacci series starts with two variables, a and b, initialized to 0 and 1. n is the limiting number for the series. The next number is the sum of the previous two numbers.

the print() function prints b, the next number in the series. The end=' ' argument to print() adds a space to the end of the list.

Finally, the print() statement adds a blank line.

To call the fib() function, to find all the Fibonacci numbers that are less than 300, call the function as follows:

```
fib(300)
```

The Run Script button runs the active script. Where did the result print? Actually, it prints on the Blender console, where all the Blender messages print. This may change in future Blender releases, but that's where it prints now.

In another text window, a simple modification to the code, in the function fib2(), returns the result as a list instead of just printing it. Instead of printing the next Fibonacci number, it is added to a list. The entire list is returned instead of being printed. Here's the code:

```
def fib2(n): # return Fibonacci series up to n
    """Return a list containing the Fibonacci series up to n."""
    result = []
    a, b = 0, 1
    while b < n:
        result.append(b)      # see below
        a, b = b, a+b
    return result

f100 = fib2(100)      # call it
print(f100)
```

The variable result is initialized to an empty list, the two square
brackets. Instead of using the print() function, the next Fibonacci
number is appended to the list using the append() method of the list
object. Finally the entire list is returned. In the call to fib2(),
the result list object is assigned to the variable f100 and then
printed.

As a final example, I would like to show you how to pass positional
and keyword arguments to a function. Positional arguments are
referenced by their position number in the argument list. Keyword
arguments have the form keyword=value. As a rule, you need to
specify all the positional arguments. The keyword arguments default
to their value, and do not have to be specified. If you do specify
them, the value you pass wll be used. A simple example, called
cubevolume, will help clarify this:

```
def cubevolume(length, width=4, height=5):
    return length * width * height


print(cubevolume(3))


#print(cubevolume(8,width=7))


#print(cubevolume())
```

The cubevolume() function calculates the volume of a cube, which is
its length, multiplied by its width, multiplied by its height. The
length argument is the only positional parameter, in the first
position. So print(cubevolume(3)) will return 60, 3 x 4 x 5.

I will uncomment print(cubevolume(8,width=7)). Running it, produces
the result 8 x 7 x 5 , or 280. The width=7 parameter overrides the
default width of 4.

Uncommenting print(cubevolume()) produces an error because the
length argument, the positional parameter, is not specified.

That's my brief introdeuction to Python 3 functions. I hope this
gets you started. Refer to the Python 3 documentation for additional
information, such as local and global variable passing in functions.